MW01299467

forgotten tales of
North Carolina

Tom Painter and Roger Kammerer

Published by The History Press
Charleston, SC 29403
www.historypress.net

Copyright © 2006 by Tom Painter and Roger Kammerer
All rights reserved

Cover art and interior line drawings by Roger Kammerer.

First published 2006
Second printing 2007

Manufactured in the United Kingdom

ISBN 978.1.59629.177.1

Library of Congress Cataloging-in-Publication Data

Painter, Tom.
forgotten tales of North Carolina / Tom Painter and Roger Kammerer.
p. cm.
ISBN 978-1-59629-177-1 (alk. paper)
1. North Carolina--History--Anecdotes. 2. North Carolina--Biography--
Anecdotes. 3. North Carolina--History, Local--Anecdotes. 4. Curiosities and
wonders--North Carolina--Anecdotes. I. Kammerer, Roger E. II. Title.
F254.6.P35 2006
975.6--dc22
2006020088

Notice: The information in this book is true and complete to the best of our knowledge. It is offered without guarantee on the part of the author or The History Press. The author and The History Press disclaim all liability in connection with the use of this book.

All rights reserved. No part of this book may be reproduced or transmitted in any form whatsoever without prior written permission from the publisher except in the case of brief quotations embodied in critical articles and reviews.

Introduction

Someone once said that "the threads that make up the skein of history are made of episodes of historical importance, the mundane and the intriguingly bizarre." It's this interest in the bizarre and the love of the unusual and long-forgotten tale that makes up the premise for this little book.

Tom Painter and I have both loved North Carolina's wonderful culture and past nearly all our lives. Tom grew up in the foothills of North Carolina and I grew up along the coast in Swansboro, North Carolina. We, like so many others, loved the endless stories of historical events and captivating yarns told to us by "old-timers" as we grew up. There have been many books published on North Carolina lore, but most retell the same stories over and over again. Having seen other amazing stories about North Carolina in our research in old records, Tom and I decided to put together a collection of these odd and unusual stories.

The stories herein are drawn from such diverse places as old newspapers and journals, court records, monuments and tales told to us by eyewitnesses, genealogists and older people we knew. They range from the mysterious to the silly and absurd. The stories deal with such things as superstitions, reminders of old ways, mysterious Indian graves, hidden walls and found treasures. There are accounts of North Carolina's famous sea monster, snakes, Big Foot and other "beasties" seen across the state. There are other accounts of comets, showers of blood, tornadoes and strange weather occurrences, as well as people who had remarkable lives and even a boy with the word "America" in his eyes.

The lover of North Carolina trivia and lore will find this book to be a treasure of intriguing subjects lost to memory and time generations ago. We believe you will enjoy this collection as much as we do.

forgotten tales of North Carolina

Dog Became Police Officer

In July 1915 "Buster," the city-owned dog of Asheville, who was a vicious rat killer around the municipal building and mascot of the fire and police stations, was nabbed by the dogcatcher for not wearing a muzzle. Learning of his plight, members of the fire and police departments went to the pound and rescued him. They bought him a muzzle and put it on him. However, Buster refused to work with a muzzle on and the firemen conceived of an idea of getting him a badge and letting him do as he pleased. The city commissioners were shown that Buster had a job for which there were no other applicants and did his job well. The firemen also reminded them that he refused to work with a muzzle on. It was immediately ordered by the city board that the muzzle law be disregarded in Buster's case and he had free reign to do his job without fear of the dogcatcher. Buster was sworn in as an officer of the law and a small policeman's badge was bought and hung from his collar.

A Snake Story

In May 1884 there was an unusual snake story making the rounds in Raleigh. It seems there was a gentleman in the northeastern part of the city, near what was Mordecai's grove, who owned a turkey hen that had a nest some distance from the house. The turkey disappeared, but after a few days turned up in a fluster. The nest was visited, when to the surprise of all it was found that a highland moccasin had taken the turkey's place and was laying upon the eggs in a most motherly manner. For some reason the snake was not killed. Five days later the cries made by young turkeys were heard, and to the astonishment of all, the snake was seen heading along a hillside with a happy brood of chicks following it. It seems the chicks hatched and the snake was imprinted as their mother.

Extraordinary Phenomenon

For centuries there have been reports of strange things falling from the sky. Some of these bizarre downfalls can be explained, while scientists choose to dismiss others for lack of knowledge. The following is one such story. On February 15, 1850, a red cloud appeared in Sampson County and there fell near the residence of Thomas M. Clark a shower of flesh and blood, about 30 feet wide and about 250 or 300 yards in length. The pieces appeared to be flesh, livers, brains and blood and appeared to be very fresh. Three of Mr. Clark's children were in the rainless shower, and ran to their mother exclaiming, "Mother there is meat falling!" Their mother immediately went to see, but the shower was over, leaving fresh blood dripping off the leaves. There were other witnesses who testified to the event and said the whole area smelled heavily of blood. Pieces of the flesh were saved and sent to two scientists in the state who verified the existence of blood but not the character of the matter. It had the smell, both in its dry state and when put in water, of putrid flesh and was adjudged as such. A very red cloud was seen over Wilmington sometime later, but nothing fell out of it.

Civil War Story

In June 1871, a New Bern newspaper reported the following strange story. It was reported that a man named Edward Brown of Pitt

County fled to the swamps during the Civil War to avoid the draft. He had lately been discovered living a hermit's life in a den and settlement of his own in a dense thicket near the banks of the Contentnea River. When first discovered he fled to his hiding place. Upon being pursued he showed fight, but finally surrendered and insisted he would not go into the army. Upon being informed that the war had ended six years earlier, he concluded to abandon his hiding place and return to the old plantation, where he found numerous changes. His only clothing was made from the skins of raccoons and other animals that he had trapped during the time. He had not seen or spoken to anyone for about eight years. He had nearly lost the control of language except for some profane words. His father and mother had both died during the previous year, believing him dead.

Love at Any Age

The following appeared in North Carolina newspapers in January 1823: "Married in Duplin County, some time since, Jacob Mathies, aged 111 years to Mrs. Sellers, aged 119 years."

Red Rabbit

It was reported in January 1888 that a man named Sid Carpenter, while hunting near Newton, North Carolina, shot and killed a natural curiosity, a red rabbit. He had it stuffed to preserve it, which caused quite a sensation among those who viewed it.

It Wasn't a Light from God

In early June 1891, an aged Methodist minister who was very bald was preaching a funeral sermon at a church in Halifax County. A restless young boy who was seated in the gallery of the church was playing with his daddy's watch. The boy adjusted the watch crystal in such a way that a beam of light from a window settled on the bald pate of the preacher. The congregation became wild with religious enthusiasm and about broke up the services with their shouting and moaning. Some thought the spirit of the deceased had descended upon the preacher, while others expected the aged pastor to be then and there raised into heaven. All the excitement alarmed the young prankster but he decided to continue his performance. Word spread far and wide about the "miracle" and continuous revivals were held in the church. After three days the young boy's trick was found out and his daddy "shore tore up his backside."

Famous North Carolinians

Most people probably have never heard of W.S. Renfrow, Hannis Taylor and Reverend Joseph C. Price. W.S. Renfrow was a native of Smithfield who enlisted in the Civil War at age sixteen in Company C, Fiftieth North Carolina Infantry. After the war his family moved to Arkansas. He moved to Oklahoma where he was a president of a bank and in 1893 was named governor of the Oklahoma

Territory. Hannis Taylor was a native of New Bern, educated at UNC-Chapel Hill and lived in Mobile, Alabama, where he was a lawyer. He was a legal author and was a practitioner before the U.S. Supreme Court. In 1893, Taylor was appointed by the president as minister to Spain. Reverend J.C. Price, described as the greatest black orator in the world, was born in Elizabeth City but raised in New Bern. He learned his letters at the age of eleven and graduated from Lincoln University and the Theological Seminary of the A.M.E. Zion Church. He was the first black man to preach in the church of Henry Ward Beecher in New York. He lectured in the leading cities across America and Europe. He was appointed by President Cleveland as consul general to Liberia, but did not accept. He was president of Livingston College from 1882 until his death in Salisbury, North Carolina, in 1893.

A Reminder of Old Ways

In former years there were in some sections of this country many who believed in witches and witchcraft. If evil befell any person or domestic animal in certain neighborhoods, the person or animal was believed to be bewitched by some enemy. It was also believed that if the image of the witch, whether a man or a woman, was carved on a tree and shot with silver bullets, the "evil spell" would be removed. This practice was once prevalent in eastern North Carolina. In April 1899, timber cutters found one such image on a cypress tree they cut down in the Lucksburg section of Sampson County, North Carolina. Nailed inside the graven image of a woman were several pieces of silver shot and a silver dime minted in 1850.

America in His Eyes

In early 1894, there was a local sensation in Greene County over a child and his unique eyes. The child was the seven-year-old son of a poor man named Mr. Lassiter, and this special boy's eyes had the word "America" imprinted around the pupil of each eye. His eyes were very dark, almost black, and the letters were a dark brown. This unusual feature was first discovered by the child's parents when he was a few months old. As he grew older the words could be seen distinctly. The boy was taken around by his father to gatherings to raise money for the family. Local newspaper editors in Greenville, Wilson and Raleigh believed the whole affair was a humbug and offered twenty-five dollars each to prove it. On an appointed day, the little boy was brought to Greenville and, in front of a crowd of curious onlookers, the editors got in the face of the little boy. They proclaimed that yes, you could see the word "America" in each eye and each gave their money to the boy's father.

Where There's a Will

In 1897, it was reported that a man from Surry County got a divorce from his wife at 9:00 a.m., walked twelve miles to his house,

got his best clothes on, walked ten miles to get a marriage license, secured it and then made the final tramp of eight miles to the home of a widow and at 9:00 p.m. married her. A man like this was bound to get a wife.

Walked on Water

In April 1898, it was reported that a man named Spence had been preaching "sanctification" in eastern Wake County and in order to carry out his religious points he announced to everyone that on the following Sunday he would walk on water. On the Saturday night prior to the big event, the preacher went to a local pond and drove in posts and laid some planks along them a few inches under the muddy water. On Sunday morning, by appointment, a large crowd assembled to see the miraculous feat. Unbeknownst to the man, some local pranksters took a late-night swim and, after discovering the setup, removed one of the planks. After spending several minutes in prayer the "sanctificationist" proceeded to walk. With eyes fixed heavenward he slowly and deliberately walked into the water. Everything was still, and such remarks as, "Gee whiz! That man sorely am sanctified!" could be heard from the eager crowd of onlookers. Suddenly, at about the middle of the pond, he came to the missing plank and ker ploosh! The parson went in over his head. The now thoroughly disgusted crowd dispersed with very little faith in sanctification.

A Loving Father

Will you be my Valentine? It is a question asked every February 14, but for Valentine A. Abernathy, he could not wait for that day of love that comes once a year. He was born on October 8, 1798, in Lincoln County. Mr. Abernathy was known for his interest in politics and the fact that he never missed a vote. It was also said that he walked fifteen miles one way just to vote, and then he would walk briskly back home immediately after. Though it seems a noble gesture, it was not the only thing that Mr. Abernathy was known for. At the age of eighty-two, he had married twice and had born to him twenty-eight children, nineteen boys and nine girls, and over four hundred great-grandchildren. Only one girl was lost, a month after her birth. He was reported to feel as spry as he had at age twenty-five and had no aches or pains.

Governor's Pay

It was reported in January 1932 that Governor O. Max Gardner had been turning back to the state treasurer 10 percent of his annual salary of $7,100. Also, the late Captain Nathan O'Berry, while state treasurer, had turned back 10 percent of his monthly check.

Unusual Names

In 1898, it was reported that there were a number of families in Rutherford County with very odd names. There was a family named Clements with children named Zeno, Zula, Zebulon, Zinnie, Zolen, Zaco, Zaluski, Zenix, Zalf and Zeolly. Another family named Andrews inflicted the following on their children: Kansas Love, Quitina Quiltina Quinn and Eulalia Valtasia Flabanico Anifecto. And yet another family named Allen disfigured their children with Linsco, Lansco and Stumpco. A few years before this report, another child near Louisburg, North Carolina, was reported to have the following names: Jesse Fido Ringtail Fillmore Hancock Jarvis Dowd Harper.

Civil War Treasure

There had long been a tale about Yankee treasure being buried in the Cameron meadow in Raleigh, but none had ever been found. In February 1898, three men named Hester, Etheridge and Stewart began digging in the meadow after work and were seen many times digging by lamplight. In early March, one of the treasure hunters, Robert Hester, found a cache of $8,000 in gold under an elm tree.

It's Always Something

It had been nearly fifty years since the Civil War closed, but the fighting spirit of some of its veterans continued on. At a Confederate reunion in Durham in May 1914, a difference arose between General J.S. Carr and Major J.M. Hamilton in regard to the parade. They got into a heated argument and slapped each other's faces. The peace spirit also followed quickly, for no sooner had their hot blood cooled down than they made up and were as good friends as ever.

Interesting Marriage

In Tarboro on February 25, 1853, at the peculiar hour of midnight, Miss Sarah Susan Elizabeth Panza Mills, daughter of Colonel

Everitt Mills, was married to Señor Don Alonzo Edgar Howard, a cosmopolite and itinerant juggler. The giddy couple was joined in the holy bonds of matrimony after a one-hour acquaintance and a "billing and cooing" courtship of fifteen minutes.

Unique Horseless Carriage

In December 1898, it was reported that an uneducated black youth in Chatham County named John Alston had made an invention that would totally revolutionize the motive power that propels machinery. He invented a "horseless carriage" or car that had an engine that was propelled by condensed air, which is more powerful than steam power. Alston's car was acclaimed by all who viewed it and in tests it ran steadily for one month. He planned to have his invention patented.

Meteorite Explosion

At about three o'clock on a Wednesday in 1849 a wonderful sight appeared over Caldwell County sky near Lenoir, North Carolina. It was a brilliant meteor headed in a southern direction approaching the earth at about a twenty- or twenty-five-degree angle from the earth's surface. Its light, which seemed whiter than the flame of fire, almost rivaled the rays of a cloudless sun, and the flash of the explosion was much more brilliant than any lightning ever witnessed. If seen at night, it would have been awfully grand, yet sublimely beautiful. When the extraordinary sight hit the earth, a great rumbling noise was heard. The terrific stone landed in Union County. Dr. Andrews of Charlotte stored the meteorite at his home in a cabinet to be viewed by the curious public. The object was said to be a combination of mineral substances in which iron appears to predominate. The weight of the stone was reported to be nineteen pounds.

Champion Fiddler

The champion fiddler of the mountains, William A. (Fiddling Bill) Hensley, died in July 1960 in Asheville. The eighty-six-year-old is remembered for fiddling at the White House during a visit of King George VI. Hensley, accompanied by his trusty fiddle, "Old Calico," appeared on the radio numerous times in New York and Texas. Six daughters and two brothers survived him at death. His last words, just before he died, were to one of his daughters. He asked her: "Did you get Old Calico?"

Remarkable Hairy Man

Reported in February 1901, Mr. Ransom Saunders of Pantego, Beaufort County, was approaching his ninetieth birthday. He was then married to his sixth wife and was the proud father of nearly forty children and still seemed to be in good health. He was said to be a hard worker who dressed very thinly even in the coldest of weather. He was not known to wear an overcoat ever. He was covered all over his person with "thick long hair," which must have been responsible for his tolerance of the cold. He was a good citizen and considered a remarkable man.

Recovered Piece of History

In 1889, Judge Schenck, who at the time was the president of the Guilford Battle Ground Company, came into the possession of a valuable and interesting relic from the old Guilford Battle Ground. It was a silver knee buckle stamped with the English coat of arms and bearing the letter "W" engraved upon it. In 1856, a great Whig mass meeting was to be held upon the old grounds and a crew of men began to clear off some of the woods. The buckle was found there on the north side of the New Garden Road along the way that Lieutenant Colonel Webster led his charge against the Continental line. It may be reasonably presumed that the costly buckle was part of his dress that day, for he was killed by a shot to the leg, which if you think about it, could have ripped the buckle from his pants. The Honorable George Davis presented the buckle to the Guilford Battle Ground Company.

A Tree Grows in Raleigh

It was reported in 1872 that there was a willow tree in Raleigh in the rear of the residence of the late John H. Bryan, which was grown from a slip taken from the willow at the grave of Napoleon, at St. Helena.

Mysterious Painful Thumb

In the summer of 1896, Mr. Pleasants, who was a Seaboard engineer, was badly scalded in a wreck at Manly, North Carolina. Due to the accident, his left hand required amputation in order to keep blood poisoning from spreading to the rest of his body. A month after the operation, Mr. Pleasants still complained to family and friends when asked if his thumb and arm pained him. He said that his hand was drawn and that his thumb was in an uncomfortable position, giving him much more annoyance. His friends laughed when hearing of his unusual pain, for they knew the hand that pained him was buried in the backyard. Mrs. Pleasants, however, being more considerate of her husband's pain, heard him mention that his thumb was drawn out of position and was clinched by the other fingers on his hand. That evening Mrs. Pleasants went out into the backyard where his hand was buried and gently dug the hand up. When she retrieved the hand, she found it to be in the same position described by her husband. The hand was clinching the thumb tightly. Mrs. Pleasants straightened the fingers on the hand and freed the paining thumb. As soon as Mrs. Pleasants entered the room where her husband was, he told her that the tendons in his arm felt free again and the paining thumb was no more. Mr. Pleasants's arm remained pain-free after that.

Larger than Life

There have been several people throughout history who were noted for their extraordinary size, and North Carolina was the birthplace of one such person. His name was Miles Darden (1799–1857). He was born near Rich Square and later moved to Madison County, Tennessee, where he was a farmer and merchant. Darden refused to be weighed after he moved to Tennessee, but his neighbors, by testing the tension on his ox wagon springs while he was aboard and then piling on rocks in another wagon for a corresponding tension, estimated his weight to be over one thousand pounds. In 1839, his coat was buttoned around three men weighing over two hundred pounds each who walked together across the square at Lexington. People reported that the giant of a man stayed active until 1843, but from that time until his death he preferred to stay at home or be hauled about in a two-horse wagon. Apparently his weight increased as his mobility decreased. In 1850, it required thirteen and a half yards of cloth one yard wide to make him a new coat. He was reported at the time of his death in January 1857 to be seven feet nine inches tall and to weigh nearly one thousand pounds. The coffin used to bury the enormous man was eight feet long, thirty-five inches deep, thirty-two inches across the breast, eighteen inches across the head and fourteen inches across the feet. Twenty-five yards of black velvet were used to cover the sides and lid. Seventeen men were required to put the body in the coffin. Mr. Darden was affirmed to have been married twice and while he had large children, they were not expected to reach half the weight of their father.

Drunken Geese

One winter during the Civil War a soldier was marching from Kinston to Swift Creek, when he stopped at an old lady's house blest with a large flock of denuded geese. It seems that there was a whiskey still near the old woman's house. One day the geese got into a tub of the homemade brew. When the old woman went out to look after her treasures, she found them laid out stone drunk. Thinking they were dead, she gathered them up, took them into the shed, picked off all their feathers and threw them off to the side of the yard. Later on the old lady heard a commotion in her yard and, when she opened her door, found a sea of naked geese. She then had to keep the birds in the house until spring.

Big Daddies

In November 1898, Riley Shepard of Indiana, age seventy-seven, returned to his native Wilkes County for a visit. He had left North Carolina about fifty years before and had outlived four wives and begat twenty-nine children and nine grandchildren. He was described as quite "spry" and intimated that he would not mind taking a fifth wife, if a suitable one could be found. He also had a brother who was the father of twenty-six children, making a combined offspring of fifty-five between them, which would make quite a family reunion. A few years before, another man in western North Carolina, named William Wellman, was said to have borne to him twenty children in only twenty-four years.

Peculiar Names

Already noted for having unusual place names, North Carolina also has a host of peculiarly named citizens, as the files of the 860,800 persons holding automobile driver's licenses in 1940 show. For instance, Worthy Money had a driver's license, as did Royal Money, Precious Worthy, Carrie Stone and Good Simons. Then there was Zero Tooten, Fake Kidd, Corn Flack and Constant Rearing. Those interested in colorful names will appreciate Rich Blue, Pine Valentine Corn, Grey Green, Pink Bridges, Lemon Ham and Pink Eagles. Other unusual names include Golden Tart, Loving Justice Good, Duck Answer, Real Jolly and Sulkie Police. Then there was

Polly Shook Leatherwood, Romance Thrower, Bold Robin Hood, Adore Coffee and Kel Paine.

Field of Dreams

In May of 1899, there was a farmer living in Halifax County who must have lived on the other side of the rainbow, for his luck materialized before his eyes. He was out plowing in his field one Saturday when the blade of his plow struck an old tin can and tore it from its ancient tomb. When the can hit the freshly turned sod, it made a jingle and rattle, catching the attention of the farmer who turned his head in time to see a glorious sight of gold coins rolling from the can. He picked up the can and found it filled with gold coins. The coins ranged in date from 1715 to 1773 and were all foreign. It was believed that the coins were buried before or during the Revolutionary War. It is estimated that the young farmer received $4,000 for the find, but he did not disclose the true amount he received for them. It was said that the farmer laughed, sang and jumped for joy upon finding the glorious cache.

Grave Stories

In August 1887, there was an unusual story out of Edgecombe County about a newly dug grave exploding. It seems a young lady had just been buried there about four days earlier when the explosion occurred. No one heard any noise, but upon investigation there was no evidence of anyone digging and the casket was not harmed. There was so much earth thrown about that it was necessary to refill the grave. The next story concerns a man who took it with him. It seems that Robert Perry of Belvidere, Perquimans County, died and was buried. After his death his family made a diligent search for his money and valuable papers, but couldn't find them. After he had been dead more than two months his family decided that the money and papers could have been in the coat of the deceased. The body was accordingly disinterred and sure enough in the inside pocket were found the papers and $500, which saved his property from sale and sacrifice.

One-ton Turtle

In June 1893 it was reported that a black turtle weighing between 1,800 and 2,000 pounds was caught near Cape Lookout. It was so large that it took fifteen men to pull it out of the water and eight men to turn it over on its back after landing. Old fishermen tell that there were larger turtles than this one caught off North Carolina shores and that this species of turtle was not fit to eat. This turtle was cooked for its valuable oil.

Blinded by the Medals

Married on April 15, 1828, at the home of Brigadier General John Waynes in Duplin County, the General to Miss Mary Merrit, of

Sampson County, after a tedious courtship of twenty-nine minutes and seven seconds.

Good Samaritan Society

In 1876, an unusual case appeared before the State Supreme Court concerning a woman with a strange grievance. She had been a member of a benevolent society in Hamilton, Martin County, known as the "Good Samaritans," which had some peculiar initiation and expulsion rites. It seems this woman had been remiss in some of her obligations and when called upon to explain, she became enraged. The heads of the association decided to perform the ceremony of expulsion, which consisted of suspending her from a piece of wood along the wall of the church by means of a rope fastened around her waist. She resisted to the extent of her ability, and after being pulled up, cried out that the rope hurt her. They let her down; her dress was torn from her and she fainted immediately. The court ruled in her favor, but the Society appealed. The ruling was overturned, judging the act one of battery, even though she was a member of that humane institution.

Squirrel Hunts

From June to August 1826, Cabarrus County became the scene of a squirrel massacre the likes of which could surely not be duplicated today. The local militia there, under the command of Captain John

Scott, was divided into two hunting parties. With a small wager between the two groups, they set out to see who could produce the largest number of squirrel skins. At the next muster meeting, the teams came together and counted the skins to determine the winner. One team managed to produce a total of 4,239 skins and the other had 3,322, amounting to a staggering 7,561 skins total. To some it may seem cruel, but at that time they felt it was a service to their community because of the scarcity of corn, a major staple at that time. They believed the varmints were capable of destroying thousands of bushels of corn and based on that assumption they felt the hunts were justified. A little over a year later, another large squirrel hunt took place on the eastern side of North Carolina. In late November 1827, twenty Edgecombe County men divided into two groups under the direction of Cullin Adams and Edmond G. Hammonds and killed 850 squirrels; Mr. Hammonds killed 94 himself. A week later, thirty-two men divided into four groups and on that day they killed 1,117 squirrels.

UFO Scare of 1897

The year 1897 was a banner year for unusual sightings in the night skies all across the country. In April 1897, an airship was reported over the city of Wilmington that sent hundreds of curious onlookers out into the streets. The "brilliant floating mass" appeared in the sky east of the city and passed over at a high rate of speed. It had some sort of searchlight that scanned over the whole city and created a sensation among the religious people in town. The airship appeared to come from the ocean and passed opposite the Market Street dock, going in the direction of the Navassa Guano works. To the naked eye, many colored lights were visible and others looking through field glasses saw some sort of upper construction. An airship of the same description was seen a few days later over Kansas City, Missouri.

GAR GAR EDWARDS

In July 1915, D.M. Clark of Greenville told a story of how he happened to be in a doctor's office there when a Mrs. E.S. Edwards of Bell Arthur, Pitt County, came in with her little boy who was not quite three years old. Having been told previously by several people that the child was an inveterate smoker, and being rather skeptical, Clark decided to wait and watch for any developments. To his great surprise the child, who could scarcely walk due to paralysis, dragged himself up to his mother and began to say, "gar, gar." Whereupon the mother produced a small cigar and after lighting it handed it to the child, like it was nothing unusual. The little fellow did not grasp the cigar with both hands as one might expect, but seized the weed between his fingers and puffed and blew his smoke in a manner that would do credit to a veteran smoker. To Mr. Clark's several questions the mother replied that the child was not quite three years old, that he was paralyzed when about twelve months old and he began smoking his father's cigar stumps soon after he was paralyzed. The boy now had to have his cigars every day to keep him quiet. The doctor also informed Mr. Clark that the child had only recovered sufficiently from his paralysis within the last month to hobble around on his feet. He did not attribute the boy's present or past condition to his tobacco habit.

Gold Mine under Main Street

In September of 1883, it was reported that Mr. Joel Reed owned a gold mine in Concord. The principal vein ran under Main Street. Mr. Reed bonded the property to a northern corporation for $10,000. The mine was located in the town, just in rear of the Methodist church. It seemed strange to the community to see the ore dumps moving and the stamp mills in operation right along one of the side streets of the town.

Unusual Gastronomics

In 1897, there was a thirty-five-year-old doctor named Gus Smith of Ironton, North Carolina, who was in one respect a most remarkable man. He was never known to drink a drop of water or to eat a bite of supper. He ate heartily at breakfast and lunch and would always drink milk.

What a Woman

There was a report that in one day in 1881, a sixty-five-year-old lady in Beaufort County picked 115 pounds of cotton, cooked three meals, went hunting and caught three coons and returned home by ten o'clock that night.

Strange Burial

In April 1888, there was a report of a strange find near Franklin, Macon County. Apparently some boys discovered some skeletons after a freshet unearthed their burial site. The skeletons, two in number, were buried in sitting positions. On the forehead of one skeleton was found a piece of solid silver, which seemed to have been worn on the front of a hat. The silver had cankered, but upon being rubbed clean there was found on it the lion and unicorn, England's coat of arms. The lion had a man's face. Under the coat of arms, on the left side, was the word "Dien" (God). On the opposite side were the words "mon droit" (my right). In a circle surrounding this symbol were the translated words "evil to him who evil thinks." In still another place was found the name Danyel Cryn, and also the date 1755. On one of the arms of the skeleton was found a solid silver bracelet about half an inch in width with no inscription. Over the breast was a piece of glass about an eighth of an inch thick and six inches square. Besides these artifacts there was found a pair of old scissors and a razor, both nearly destroyed by rust, some buckles and a number of small white beads and some flax cloth. About two hundred yards upriver was one of the best-preserved Indian mounds at the time. The skeletons were of European origin and were possibly buried by the Indians in their manner.

Whiteville's Underground River

News was received in 1888 that the town of Whiteville in Columbus County possessed a great sensation within its town limits. The roaring and rushing sound of water could be plainly heard from below the earth and if you were to lie flat upon the ground, the phenomenon became very alarming. The sound seemed to be just under the surface and it was not believed to be a small stream. Wagons passed over the ground where the phenomenon existed, creating an echo under the ground. It sounded as if there was a cavern beneath the earth. The people of Whiteville possessed a morbid curiosity of the mystery and hundreds of people had visited the spot. The community feared that the bottom might fall out of the whole town and it would fall into the hole.

The Monkey Fiddler

In 1875, an old man from the swamps of Hyde County told an unusual story from his youth about a poor musician and his pet monkey. It seems the musician had trained his monkey to act like he was playing a fiddle. During a fit of depression the poor musician hanged himself one night with a cord made by twisting together a number of fiddle strings. At the moment the man committed the act, his pet monkey jumped on his back and with his master's bow played the cord. The monkey created such a racket as to wake up everyone in the house, and thus the fiddler was cut down in time to save his life.

Barter Extravaganza

In February 1904 there was a curious story out of Currituck County about a man named Outlaw who traded his wife and two children to his brother for a pair of fishing nets, the exchange being agreeable to all parties concerned. After the trade Jerome Outlaw, to whom the woman and children were given, was arrested for the trade in Elizabeth City. The man and woman were taken to Currituck for trial, but in view of the fact that there was not sufficient evidence to convict them and that the children of the defendants were dependent on someone for support, the couple was released. The brother with the fishing nets was shrewd enough to know that his presence would only breed trouble, so he disappeared. Presumably he was putting the nets to good use.

Old Man

In April 1898 Noah Raby, an inmate of the Piscataway township almshouse near New Brunswick, New Jersey, celebrated his 126th birthday. He claimed he was born in Eatontown, Gates County, North Carolina, on April 1, 1772. He said his mother was from South Carolina and his father was a North American Indian. He had been an inmate of the almshouse for forty years and was strong and healthy except for being partially blind.

Inventor of the Revolver

It is a little-known fact that New Bern was the home of the famous inventor of revolvers, John Gill. He was a mechanical engineer with only three months' education. He invented the revolver in 1829, later inventing such things as the use of wax in making fake fruit and flowers, non-slip boots and numbers of other interesting gadgets.

A Whopper

In June 1875 the capture of an eel weighing over one hundred pounds and measuring more than twenty feet long was reported from Beaufort. Fishermen among some sound flats discovered the eel and they drove a pole through its tail to capture it. A wooden tank was constructed to hold the eel so that it could be sent to Raleigh for exhibition, but it died soon after.

Coastal Giant

The coast of North Carolina once had a giant named Lewis Lewark, son of John Lewark, a fisherman on Albemarle Sound. In 1904, Lewis was twenty-one years old and weighed 710 pounds. When he was in grade school he weighed 500 pounds and his mother informed others that he weighed 150 pounds before he

The Treasure of Bladenboro

In 1869, a very curious discovery was made in a small islet situated in Big Swamp, Bladen County, about six or seven miles from Bladenboro, the particulars of which are as follows. In the spring of 1806 there appeared on the eastern edge of the swamp an Englishman by the name of Elias Hugo. He appeared to be about thirty-eight years old, and although his language and bearing denoted that he had been educated, he bore the unmistakable evidence of a hard life. He built himself a cabin and chose to seek a cheerless and secluded life. The cabin fronted the swamp and from his front door led a narrow walk to the swamp; then, turning in a westerly direction, the path led a narrow was weaned. Lewis exhibited himself sometimes, going to Virginia Beach and Norfolk, but was afraid of venturing too far from home. He slept on an iron bed and had a huge chair constructed for his use. He spent all his time on the beach fishing with his father.

Young Bridegroom

In September 1859, there was married in Davie County Mr. John Fine, age ninety-six, to Miss Elizabeth Harley of Davidson, age thirty-seven. This interesting couple walked eight miles to the home of the magistrate to be married, and after dinner Fine had a merry time with jests and stories entertaining the large crowd who had assembled to witness the ceremony, and they then walked the eight miles back home.

What Goes Around

When he joined the war in 1861 at the age of eighteen, Mr. Calvin Dellinger's mother gave him a gold dollar. He carried the coin all through the four years of battle and when he came home he gave it back to her. In July 1898 in Lincolnton, the same dollar came back to him in a subscription to a church building fund.

INVENTOR OF THE REVOLVER

It is a little-known fact that New Bern was the home of the famous inventor of revolvers, John Gill. He was a mechanical engineer with only three months' education. He invented the revolver in 1829, later inventing such things as the use of wax in making fake fruit and flowers, non-slip boots and numbers of other interesting gadgets.

A WHOPPER

In June 1875 the capture of an eel weighing over one hundred pounds and measuring more than twenty feet long was reported from Beaufort. Fishermen among some sound flats discovered the eel and they drove a pole through its tail to capture it. A wooden tank was constructed to hold the eel so that it could be sent to Raleigh for exhibition, but it died soon after.

COASTAL GIANT

The coast of North Carolina once had a giant named Lewis Lewark, son of John Lewark, a fisherman on Albemarle Sound. In 1904, Lewis was twenty-one years old and weighed 710 pounds. When he was in grade school he weighed 500 pounds and his mother informed others that he weighed 150 pounds before he

Barter Extravaganza

In February 1904 there was a curious story out of Currituck County about a man named Outlaw who traded his wife and two children to his brother for a pair of fishing nets, the exchange being agreeable to all parties concerned. After the trade Jerome Outlaw, to whom the woman and children were given, was arrested for the trade in Elizabeth City. The man and woman were taken to Currituck for trial, but in view of the fact that there was not sufficient evidence to convict them and that the children of the defendants were dependent on someone for support, the couple was released. The brother with the fishing nets was shrewd enough to know that his presence would only breed trouble, so he disappeared. Presumably he was putting the nets to good use.

Old Man

In April 1898 Noah Raby, an inmate of the Piscataway township almshouse near New Brunswick, New Jersey, celebrated his 126th birthday. He claimed he was born in Eatontown, Gates County, North Carolina, on April 1, 1772. He said his mother was from South Carolina and his father was a North American Indian. He had been an inmate of the almshouse for forty years and was strong and healthy except for being partially blind.

track to the islet. Here in his secluded abode, alone and uncared for, Hugo lived until his death on May 13, 1809. After his death, strange stories were told of a specter that was seen and of strange sounds that were heard about the house and premises, and so deeply had a superstitious dread of the place taken hold upon the minds of the locals that the cabin was permitted to decay and fall. In early 1869, the place fell into the possession of Joel H. Ester and son. They immediately set about clearing away the remains of the old cabin. They had not proceeded far, however, before they discovered, on raising the floor, a small tin box snugly encased in the base of the chimney under the hearth. The box was some eighteen or twenty inches square and made of very thick tin. It contained a copy of Raphael's *Madonna*, a small cross and a razor with the initials "H.H." nicely engraved on the handle, nine hundred livres and the following abstracted letter:

Bladen Co., N.C. May 11, 1809
To Samuel W. Hugo
Cheapside, London, England
My dear brother, this is perhaps the last address I shall ever send you…Come to America, as I urged you in a previous letter. I have buried all the money I brought with me, amounting to about one Million, three hundred thousand dollars, on a small islet nearby, the directions to which I have already sent you. The amount is contained in seven different boxes, and is buried in separate places on the islet.

Your affectionate brother,
Elias Hugo

So, whatever became of the treasure? Maybe someone with a little ingenuity and research could come up with it.

POLITICAL DEATH

It was reported in a northern newspaper that there was an unusual affray over the proposed Constitution of the United States in Dobbs County on April 13, 1788, which proved fatal to nearly all its participants. It seems the fracas was between Colonel Sheppard and William Barfield, who fell into a heated dispute over the Constitution. Colonel Sheppard, being irritated with Mr. Barfield, proceeded to strike him with his horsewhip, at which an apprentice boy of Mr. Barfield's took up a broad axe and struck Colonel Sheppard on the cheek, severely cutting the side of his face and breaking his collarbone. A nephew of Colonel Sheppard who happened to be present wrestled the axe away from the youth, who then took his master's rifle and shot at Colonel Sheppard's nephew, wounding him in both arms, one of which later had to be amputated. Colonel Sheppard died a few days later from his wounds.

FREE LUNCH

In June 1932, H.L. Langley of the Bettie community of Carteret County had an unusual experience. He was working in his field one morning when out of the clear blue sky a four-pound speckled trout fell at his feet. Taking advantage of the gift from above, Mr. Langley delivered the fish, still living, to his kitchen to be his free lunch.

Married His Sister

In December 1895 at Chestnut Hill, near Salisbury, Miss Prudy Hopkins and Mr. John Pennington were married. This would not be unusual except the bride's father and the groom's mother were husband and wife, which made the young folks stepbrother and sister. So by marrying her stepbrother the bride becomes her own sister-in-law and the daughter-in-law of her own father and the groom becomes his own brother and the stepson-in-law of his own mother.

Strange Fish

In May 1876, a strange fish creature was brought to the Market Wharf at Washington. This fish creature was described as having a long round body about two feet in length, mouth like a hog, feet like an alligator, stripes like a snake and ears covered in downy hair. It was caught in the Pamlico River and even the oldest fishermen could not tell what it was. In July 1919, Zeph Potts and Tom Robbins were surf fishing at Hatteras Inlet. Potts had about one hundred feet of line out and was quietly wading through the surf when he suddenly felt a strike on his line. So fierce was the pull on his line that it yanked him off his feet and buried his nose in the sand. He managed to regain his balance and fought the fish for over half an hour before succeeding in landing it. The fish was of a nature never before seen on the island. It measured seven feet from stem to stern and was striped almost like a zebra. It had long ears, which is unusual for a fish, and the teeth in its mouth were formed almost exactly like those of a human being. In addition to a large tail it had two smaller tails on each side of the big one. After being exhibited no one could say what kind of fish it was.

Unusual Find

There was exhibited in New Bern in September 1889 a curiosity in the shape of what looked like an elephant tusk. On a card attached to the object were these words: "This tusk was taken by Richard Midyette, while fishing a drag net at New Inlet Pamlico Sound, N.C." It looked like ivory, was two feet five inches in length, two and a half inches in diameter at the larger end and with a slight curve tapered gracefully to a point. It weighed nearly four and a half pounds.

Raleigh Black Woman a Confederate Pensioner

In June 1930, the beloved "Aunt Jane" Robinson, the only black woman on the North Carolina Confederate pension roll, died at the Wake County Home at the age of one hundred. Aunt Jane, a picture from the past, was once a familiar figure on the streets of Raleigh, having been employed in her active years by the Colonel Charles E. Johnson and Briggs families. According to Henry M. London, who knew her well, Jane had a clear memory of the troops marching away to the Mexican War eighty-three years before. At the suggestion of Colonel Bryan Grimes, former secretary of state, a bill was prepared by Mr. London and passed by the North Carolina legislature in 1921 placing Jane on the pension rolls. Her husband was a bodyguard of Captain John Nichols of the First North Carolina Cavalry and was killed while accompanying his master at the battle of Manassas Gap. During the Civil War Aunt Jane washed and ironed for soldiers in the Pettegrew Hospital, which became Peace Institute.

Beach Sand Clock

In June 1887, Mr. S.F. Tieser, a merchant in New Bern, wanted to go on an excursion to Morehead City. Before he left he consulted a physician about going into the sea. The physician told him it would do him good to go in the surf, provided he would not stay in over fifteen minutes. Wishing to observe scrupulously the instructions of his doctor and fearing to risk getting saltwater in his watch, he took a large-sized clock with him on the beach. He placed the clock dial facing the ocean so that he could tell when to get out.

Royal Connections

In the early 1900s, Virginia Harding, a native of Raleigh, was the wife of Baron Strade d'Ekna, Swedish minister to Austria. Her granddaughter, Countess Geraldine Apponzi of Hungary, married on April 27, 1938, in Tirana, Albania, to King Zog of Albania. In Berlin, Germany, it was announced that Chancellor Adolph Hitler sent King Zog an automobile bearing the Albanian royal coat of arms and also a helmet of the Albanian national hero, Skanerberg, as a wedding present.

Pea-loving Eels

In October 1889 there was a peculiar tale from the Catawba River. A man who often brought eels to market told a story about how he had seen numerous eels early in the morning leaving his pea patch he had on the riverbank, where no doubt they had been feasting. Another local farmer from Catawba County backed up this narrative with a similar episode. It seems he was plowing in a creek bottom one day and had his dog with him. The dog was a great snake chaser, and on this particular day began barking at something about 150 yards from the creek. Upon investigation, he found it to be a live eel.

A Singular Marriage

In 1857, an unusual marriage took place in Wilkes County. A man named Holloway married his stepmother, his father's second wife. The woman had six children, three by the father and three illegitimate ones by Holloway. Since the younger Holloway had nine children of his own, the couple set up house with fifteen children, all with unusual kinship.

Bigfoot in North Carolina?

On at least two different occasions in the nineteenth century in North Carolina, stories of a "hairy wild man" were reported. The first encounter was in February of 1878 near Blowing Rock. Several gentlemen were prospecting for gold in Globe Valley. Far from any human habitation they suddenly became aware of a large "hairy manlike creature" some forty yards in the distance. Overwhelmed with curiosity, they walked toward the beast for a better look. They were able to get within sixty feet of it and stopped again to see its reaction. Even at that distance the beast seemed to be a giant. One of the men jumped toward it and yelled out. The creature stepped toward the men a few steps, paused and began to pound on its chest with its large fists. After the creature's show of fearlessness, it remained paused for a few more minutes. Without warning the creature turned and ran away from the mob with the speed of a deer. The men went back to the nearest house they could find and armed themselves, then returned to the valley to search for the creature. They spent the rest of the day searching the area for it but came up empty-handed. They did, however, discover a small cave near Blowing Rock that contained a bed of leaves and several bones thought to belong to opossums. They believed the cave to have been the home of the creature for many years. The creature was described to be around six and a half feet tall, broad-shouldered, with long "apish arms." His face was smooth and he had a "funnel-shaped head." His body was covered with dark brown hair about two inches long and his head was covered with long, dark red tresses of hair. The second encounter with a similar creature

took place near Raleigh in August of 1887. Mr. Pierce Howell reported to have seen the "varmint" on his property. He stated that it appeared to be a "grown gorilla" and that it had a young one with it. Others claimed it was a large bear or a wild hairy man. After the sighting, hunters covered the area searching for it, but it could not be found.

Wife Abuse

There once was a man named Warren Evans who lived in Goldsboro. In July 1873, he and his wife of 220 pounds got into a fight and she "endeavored to give him a funeral at his expense." She tied him to a fence and "fondled him" with seasoned timber, after which she "put him to sleep" with a chair. When he awoke he grew inquisitive and wished to ascertain at what period he might expect a cessation of hostilities. Mrs. Evans responded by knocking him down and gratified his curiosity by picking him up and knocking him down again for variety. She then "frescoed" his head with a lightwood knot, after which she scoured his eyes with a shovel of dirt and rolled him under the house. When the episode ended the unfortunate Evans looked like an animated chessboard.

Cat Heaven

Everyone knows that horses run wild on the Core banks along the coast, but did you know cats did too? It was reported in 1915 that the beach between Lookout and Portsmouth was probably the only place in the world where cats of the ordinary backyard kind ran wild. Fishermen reported hundreds of cats of every description among the dunes. They got there probably due to mainlanders who for years ferried them over to the beach and turned them loose because of their superstition against harming cats.

His Own Grandfather

In 1879, a young man from Johnston County explained how he was his own grandfather. It seems that he married a widow who had a grown-up daughter. His father visited his house often and fell in love with the stepdaughter and married her. So as the young mans put it, "My father became my son-in-law, and my stepdaughter my mother, because she married my father. Sometime afterward my wife had a son. He is my father's brother-in-law and my uncle, because he is the brother of my stepmother. Then my father and stepmother had a son. This made the son my brother and at the same time my grandchild, for he is the son of my daughter. My wife is my grandmother because she is [my] mother's mother. I am my wife's husband and grandchild at the same time; and as the husband of a person's grandmother is his grandfather, I am my own grandfather!"

Black Hail

In May 1901 there was a report of a large hailstorm near Ayden, Pitt County, which produced black hail. It was described as "muddy and black looking" and a number of pieces were an inch and half in diameter. The hail was nearly eighteen inches deep in some places.

Instant Family

In 1887, J.W. Culbreth of Harnett County said he was the only man in the state who could boast of five children born in wedlock in one year. In January 1887 his wife had twins and in December 1887 she had triplets.

Prison Candy

In December 1927 George Ross Pou, superintendent of the state prison, placed an order for 1,700 pounds of mixed candies. Superintendent Pou had for several years given each prisoner a pound of candy on Christmas Day, plus a bag of mixed nuts, an orange and an apple. In addition to these "extras," each prisoner was given as much chicken stew as he could eat and a quarter of a pie.

Unusual Migration

In September 1927 there was a strange report of thousands upon thousands of sand fiddlers in a mighty migration across the beach south of Cape Hatteras. Where they came from was a mystery, but they were headed for the surf. Behind them a drove of hogs trotted, dining off the stragglers. The hogs followed the sand crabs into the water, continuing to eat while standing to their shoulders in the surf. Witnesses to this unusual spectacle said the air was full of the sound of clashing claws as the creatures moved seaward.

Ninety-nine Grandchildren

In October 1897 a man named Daniel Miller, age eighty-four, lived near the Wilkes County line. He had twenty-one children and ninety-nine grandchildren. It was his hope that God would let him live to see his one hundredth.

Strange Find

In January 1878 a crew of men were opening a marl bed on the farm of A. Case in Pitt County when they struck into what was supposed to be a small creek, some six or eight feet below the surface. To their astonishment they found an Indian canoe with skeletal remains sitting upright, with the remnant of a paddle in his hands. It was supposed that in some earlier times the embankment must have given away and buried the poor fellow. Throngs of citizens as far away as Raleigh came out to look and puzzle at the discovery.

Industrious Woman

In 1888 there lived in Philadelphia an ingenious woman known as Mrs. Maria E. Beasley. Her maiden name was Hauser and she was a native of Forsythe County. She resided in New Bern for many years, where she ran a millinery business. Later she patented many remarkable inventions, including a baking pan, two barrel-making machines, a lifesaving raft for steamships and a powerful fire extinguisher for fire engines with an attachment for saving people from burning buildings.

Boss Ride

It was reported in September 1889 that a young man named Edward Stephens, living in Henderson, made a trip to Newark, New Jersey, a distance of 533 miles, on a bicycle in fifteen days.

Historical Fact

It is a little-known fact that James Burney, a native of Craven County, discovered the universally renowned giant trees of Calaveras County, California. The grove of giant trees became known as the Burney Grove in his honor, after he discovered them in 1848 while in command of a party of soldiers chasing marauding Indians. Many of the trees are close to three thousand years old.

Muskrat War

In 1883 there were numerous reports of herds of muskrats on the seashore along the outer banks of North Carolina. In May 1883 D. Etheridge and E.T. Owens, members of the lifesaving service, while on their patrol from lifesaving station No. 10, were attacked by the muskrats. After a desperate fight in which he received a slight wound on his leg, Owens was compelled to retreat. Etheridge killed several of them. There were other reports of like incidents by other patrolmen. Why the muskrats left their freshwater home in droves was a mystery. Later muskrats attacked patrolman T.M. Snow on horseback. The horse became frightened and threw Snow, after which another desperate fight ensued, leaving a number of muskrats dead. In another incident, surf man D.M. Tate was on duty at station No. 12 at night when he saw something coming at him at great speed. He struck at it several times and it plunged into the surf. A campaign was launched to exterminate the beach muskrats, which brought to light some huge ones. In April of 1883 Red Anderson and David Wilkinson, Esquire, killed a muskrat weighing forty-five pounds at Nebraska in Hyde County. After several shots the animal was dispatched.

Continuous Fires

In 1898, it was reported that there was a man named Daniel Root near Shelby, North Carolina who had a fire in his fireplace that

had been burning for 75 years. He was then about eighty years old, lived in the same house he was born in and had always raised his foodstuffs and wore homespun clothes. In 1938, there was another story of a man named William Morris, of Polk County, who had a fire that had been burning for over 150 years. Morris and his fire gained national attention and he appeared on the NBC radio program *We the People*, telling how he kept the fire, which was started by his ancestors, burning in his log cabin.

Unwelcome Guests

In February 1932, Mr. G.A. Jones, a newspaper editor, was driving near Goldsboro when suddenly an owl flew though the open windshield of his car holding a long black snake in its claws. After flopping the snake over the head and face of the driver, the owl settled on the backseat of the car, still holding the snake. No wreck ensued, but the editor, a one-armed man, lost no time in stopping the car and getting out quickly. After due consideration, he cautiously opened the back door and shooed out the undesirable occupants.

THE WITCH OF GOOSE CREEK ISLAND

The following tale was told in 1899 by Reverend H.S. Davenport, one of the most prominent ministers in the Christian church in the state. To say the least, it is a strange story.

> *Mr. Witch was hard pressed for a ride when he selected an old woman fifty years of age for his horse and committed a most ruthless act when he hitched her to the head of a grave marker. But nevertheless witches have always been credited with doing unusual things. The story came from Goose Creek Island, North Carolina, where there lived an eighty-four-year-old man named Benson Lewis, who was an intelligent and respected citizen. His family consisted of his wife, fifty, and a daughter, seventeen. Some time in 1898, bricks began to be hurled in his yard and at his house. One night a wooden window was found to be knocked in with his own axe. Among other missiles hurled in his yard was a rock weighing about eight pounds. Mr.*

Lewis suspected someone was annoying him for some purpose or some supposed slight. One night he stayed up and fired his gun in the direction he thought the missiles came, but no one was detected. Neighbors came at night and witnessed as bricks and rocks were hurled at his house, but still no one could be seen.

One day when the old gentleman and his wife were in a field near their locked house, they were startled by the sound of stamping in the house. They rushed to their house, opened the door and found no one inside, but impressions were found on the floor resembling the hoof prints of a small colt. Numerous people saw the prints but no explanation could account for them. Soon after, the wife told of being ridden three times by a witch. A neighbor expressed a desire to see her after the second ride under the witches' saddle. The lady was one of the best women of the place and no one acquainted with her would doubt her truthfulness. A few days after she expressed her wish, Mrs. Lewis's daughter came running to the lady's house at an early hour saying the witch had ridden her mother again. They both ran a quarter of a mile back to the Lewis house where Mrs. Lewis was discovered lying partly on two beds, making a noise like the groaning of a horse and her legs, arms and face covered with mud. Her gown was muddy and all knotted behind. Her hair was plaited in small and large plaits. Mrs. Lewis claimed the "witch" was a man, that he rode her several miles, drove her to a graveyard and tied her to the head board of a grave of a newly buried child. Upon investigation, the grave she spoke of was found and it was that of a child who had been dead only two weeks.

No one seemed to have an idea who the witch was, but it created a sensation in the area. Some thought it was a trick of Mr. Lewis's wife. But then she could not have made the racket in the house while she was with her husband in the field. She also could not have thrown objects at the house in the presence of witnesses. People were there and watched both day and night as invisible hands threw bricks and rocks. The missiles did not hit anyone and seemed to drop from above and strike with considerable force, often breaking the brick in to pieces.

Nothing more is known of what happened to the Lewis family and the witch of Goose Creek Island.

Finders Keepers

In 1857, Mr. Benjamin Dey of Currituck County was certainly a lucky man when an old pine tree fell in one of his fields, obstructing the plowing that was in progress. One of the limbs of the tree was forced deep into the earth. When the workers pulled the limb from its hole, it was observed to have coins stuck within its bark. They immediately went to work digging at the hole to see if there was more where that came from. After digging about four feet into the earth the treasure was spotted. It took a yoke of oxen to pull the wealth from the earth. The treasure consisted of Spanish gold and silver coins that were once the coin of choice in the colonies of America up until the mid-nineteenth century. After it was counted, the treasure amounted to about $6,000. If Mr. Dey was not a wealthy man at the time he surely was after that discovery. The treasure, suspected to be buried around the time of the Revolution, left some to wonder if some pirate possibly had his hand in it some years before.

Old Soldier

It was reported in June 1894 that David McCoy, a hale and hearty gentleman of San Bernadino County, California, and a pensioner of the War of 1812, was 104 years old. It was said he fought in the battle of Thames River, where he witnessed the death of Tecumseh, the Indian ally of the British. Mr. McCoy was born in Burke County, North Carolina, on May 2, 1790, a year after Washington's inauguration. His father was a Scotsman who fought in the British army during the Revolution, but who refused to reenlist after his time had expired and escaped to the wilds of North Carolina.

Siam Connection

There was a Dr. W.A. Cheek, a native of Orange County, who went to Bangkok, Siam, and entered into a partnership with the Siamese government in the teak lumber industry. After a time, the Siamese government alleged he defaulted in his contract. Cheek's property, which consisted largely of a vast herd of elephants that were used to transport the teak, was seized and he died later after having vainly endeavored to secure justice at the hands of the Siamese officials. The widow of Dr. Cheek and her children returned to Hillsborough, North Carolina, and the American consul and the Siamese government battled it out in court. An arbitrator was brought in and in April 1898, the arbitrator ruled in favor of the Cheek estate, which was to receive $200,000.

Unlucky Horseshoe

It has long been said that if you found a horseshoe in the road and carried it home and nailed it up over the door you would have good luck. Not so for a Greenville, North Carolina, man in 1897. It seems one day this man found a horseshoe in the street and proudly went home to nail it up. After reaching his home he made preparations to nail it over the door in the presence of an interested group of spectators consisting of his wife and three small children. No sooner had he struck the nail for the first time than the hammer slipped from his grasp and fell on his youngest child's head. After dealing with this episode, he climbed the ladder again to continue. At the second stroke of the hammer he missed the nail, hit his thumb and in the excitement and verbal tirade of the moment, pushed the stepladder over, mixing the rest of his family up on the floor. After gathering himself together and more bad words, he picked up the horseshoe and threw it out the window. Within a minute the next-door neighbor came over to complain that the iron missile had struck her pet dog on the back and it was having a fit and might not recover. The man vowed that the next time he found a horseshoe he would advertise for its owner in six newspapers.

THE CLAY-EATERS OF EDGECOMBE COUNTY

In the 1920s there were reports that there were people in eastern North Carolina who would eat clay. It was not unusual to see groups of families digging clay in the Old Sparta section of Edgecombe County every day. When asked by passersby as to what they were doing with the clay, they were told they were planning to bake and eat it. Local doctors said that they believed the clay-eaters received some kind of nutrition or minerals from the clay that their bodies craved, but it had a terrible effect on their digestive systems. Doctors in the area still dealt with clay eating way up into the 1960s.

A CORPSE SPEAKS

In April 1920, there was a tale out of Portsmouth, Carteret County, which bordered on a miracle. It seemed a Mrs. Emmeline Dixon, age seventy, lapsed into what her family thought was death. She had been in bad health for some time and for a person of her age to pass away quietly was not unusual. Her remains were reviewed and everyone accepted her condition as death, since her body became rigid and her complexion was deathly pale. She was prepared for burial, a casket sent for and the "corpse" was laid therein. A crowd of friends and relatives from the neighborhood came and "sat up" with the body, as was customary. The local traveling Methodist minister was engaged by the family and the next morning he arrived to preach the funeral. In the presence of a large crowd the minister performed the last sad rites for Mrs. Dixon and, with the assistance of others, was in the act of placing the casket lid on when the "dead" woman spoke saying, "Please don't put the cover on just now." Everyone was dumbfounded for a moment and some ran from the house in a frightened state at the strange occurrence. Mrs. Dixon was immediately removed from the casket and placed under medical care. At the last report she was rapidly gaining strength, with no explanation for the strange episode.

Old Tuning Fork

In November 1916, Reverend P.P. Orr of the Boyleston section near Sylvan, North Carolina, was showing off probably the oldest tuning fork in this part of the country. Orr said it was about two hundred years old, and he used it in all his song services when he didn't have an organ or piano. He said that Billy Walker of Spartanburg, a pioneer Christian harmony teacher, brought the instrument from England. It later passed into the hands of Wash Hamilton and then into Mr. Orr's possession forty-five years before.

A Young Grandmother

There was a report in 1893 that a young woman named Rozetta Hinton living near Princeton was a grandmother before she was twenty-seven years old. She was under thirteen when her daughter was born, and this daughter became a mother before she was fourteen.

More Large Snakes

In July 1898, Colonel John C. Hope, a man who captured rattlesnakes in tow sacks and brought them to market in Lincolnton, reported that he killed at High Shoals a rattler 6 feet 2½ inches long, 18 inches in circumference and with eighteen rattles. It was said to be the largest snake killed in that section. In August 1887 a woman from Murphy awoke in the night to find a large snake coiled around her neck. Instead of fainting, she grabbed the reptile and flung it against the wall with all her force and went to sleep again. Daylight revealed one of the largest dead rattlers ever seen in that vicinity.

Applause Leader

Things were said to be lively at a county convention in Kinston in April 1902. It seemed Mr. H.E. Shaw, a speaker at the convention, brought his little dog with him. During the speech by his master the dog had a fleabite and he began to scratch. His hind leg struck the floor every time he got at the place the flea was doing business. The members at the convention heard the tapping and thought someone was applauding the speech, so they took it up and heartily applauded. It took some time for Mr. Shaw to get through his speech, but it was enthusiastically received.

Meteors in Pitt County

In February 1935 a fragment of rock crossed the heavens and fell with a deafening crash in the woods on the farm of J.E. Jones near St. John's Church, about seven miles southeast of Ayden, Pitt County. The next morning two youths found the impact site and recovered a twenty-five-pound rock. It was said to look like any other mass of molten rock, but it had crevices lined with a golden-looking substance. The meteor was carried to the home of Mr. Jones for safekeeping. It was said that this was the second meteor to crash in this territory during the past six months. The first meteor produced a huge flash and detonation near Kinston and fragments fell near Farmville and a large fragment struck a barn at Hookerton. The fragment recovered near Farmville was given to the State Museum.

Ancient Craftsman

It was reported in September 1889 that there was a black man named Joe McKethan, aged 116 years, who was the best basket maker in Cumberland County. It was said that he regularly walked the twenty miles to Fayetteville and back in one day.

THE BACKWARD SNAKE

In 1893 Mr. G.J. Ipock, who owned a mill on Swift Creek, Craven County, told of a curious sight that he witnessed while in his boat. It was a water moccasin that had captured a live catfish. The snake had his mouth shut fast on the fish and was crawling "backward" up an inclined bank with it. Mr. Ipock struck at the snake with a piece of wood and the snake released the fish, which rolled down the embankment into the river. The snake also plunged into the river. Mr. Ipock said this was his first knowledge that a snake could go any way except forward.

A GOOD EGG

It has been said that an egg laid on Good Friday will not spoil, but simply dry up. The same has also been said for eggs laid on Easter Sunday. In 1892, Moses Roberts of New Bern made a test of the matter by keeping an egg that had been laid on Easter for a year. On breaking it open on Easter Sunday 1893, he was surprised to see that it had neither spoiled nor dried up, but retained every indication of a fresh-laid egg. Whether it was a mere happenstance with this egg or not, the incident was remarkable.

Shower of Rocks

In 1880 there was a report of an unusual incident witnessed many years before on the farm of Jacob Parker, near Statesville. It seems from a cloudy sky there came a sudden shower of stones and rocks that nearly killed the livestock on the farm.

The Nude Man

There was an unusual story in 1911 about a strange man named John Castollow, sixty-one years old, who lived four miles east of Windsor. He was hale, hearty and happy without ever wearing a stitch of clothing and could not speak a word except the monosyllable "gee," which he used in varied intonations to express himself. His caretakers and visitors said he was entirely nude with a normal, well-shaped body, but possessed extraordinary strength. It was said he could break a double plow-line as easily as if it were a cotton cord. He was described as a gentle man who was never known to intentionally hurt a living soul.

The Smallest Post Office

In 1954, when it closed after sixty years service, the post office of Grimeshawes had the distinction of being the smallest in the United States. It was a log-trimmed building about four by five feet square. It was operated year-round by postmistress Mrs. Dewey Passmore and offered full postal services such as parcel post, registered mail and money orders. It served about ten families and summer vacationers.

Saved by Annoyance

In 1933 an annoying clock and a woodpecker saved two different North Carolina residents from possible death after their homes caught fire. In Scotland Neck, Isaac Smith awoke one night, much annoyed by the constant pecking of a woodpecker. Fed up, he dressed and went downstairs only to find the back part of his house in flames. In Washington, T.R. Hodges, a light sleeper, woke up when a clock in his room stopped ticking. He got up to wind the clock and noticed a glare outside his window. Upon investigation he too found the rear of his house on fire.

Proud of Their Product

In the 1930s, labeled bootleg whiskey found its way to the illegal markets of North Carolina, although eastern North Carolina was long known for its moonshine. Two labeled brands that were widely known were Hidden Valley and East Lake Rye. The label on the back of the twelve-ounce bottle of Hidden Valley read: "Notice—Not bottled in bond. This product is guaranteed 100 percent pure 100 proof. We ask our representatives to stand behind our product." The main label announced in prominent type, "Pure Hidden Valley rye, aged in wood, six months old, manufactured by Valley Distributing Corporation, State of Virginia." The other labeled bootleg brand, East Lake Rye, only had the name on the label with an Indian with his hand leveled over his eyebrows peering into the distance.

Lost Colony Relics?

In September 1911 it was reported that the ruins of an Indian village had been unearthed near Nag's Head and many unique relics had been found. The most remarkable things found were a plate and saucer covered in English designs.

Venerable Old Man

In 1902, there lived in Halifax County an elderly black man named Ely Pitt who claimed to be 104 years old. He said he remembered well when "the stars fell." He was looked upon as a medicine man and he wore skins of rabbits, squirrels, foxes and the like on his cap and had skins sewn on his clothes.

Mystery of the English Medallion

During the fall of 1943, Leonard Holliday, a former Martin County commissioner, was in the midst of logging operations on the Roanoke River in the lower part of Martin County. One morning while walking through the swamp, he noticed an object in the mud. He stuck it in his pocket and after cleaning it later the object turned out to be a copper medallion awarded to the Duke of Cumberland by the English Parliament after the 1746 battle of Culloden. If this medallion was the original or a replica, how did it get lost in the mud of a river swamp? And where is it now?

The Mattamuskeet Apple

According to story, back in colonial days, one George Williams who lived near Lake Mattamuskeet went over to the ocean beach to a wrecked ship that had come ashore in a storm. The beach was covered with apples that had floated ashore from the wreck. Williams gathered up a large sack of apples and carried them home with him. From the seeds of these apples planted along Lake Mattamuskeet by George Williams sprang the celebrated and favorite winter Skeet apple.

Big Family

In August 1899 Mrs. Kate Medaris, aged 101 years old, died in Brooklyn, Indiana. She was born in North Carolina on June 24, 1798. She left 130 living descendants: 2 sons, 30 grandchildren, 82 great-grandchildren, 15 great-great-grandchildren and one great-great-great-grandson, born to Mr. and Mrs. Orval Beler at Friendswood, Indiana, on March 10, 1899.

The Freeze of 1780

During the winter of 1780, a long cold spell is said to have frozen over the Trent and Neuse Rivers. At and above New Bern, persons crossed and re-crossed on the ice at pleasure, both night and day. The ice was so thick on the Neuse River that cattle and horses crossed with no problem. It was also said that Sheriff Williams gave several dances or "balls" to commemorate the freeze on the north side of the Neuse at the Core Point Ferry House, later known as Pettifer's landing. Large numbers of ladies and gentlemen from New Bern walked or sleighed over the ice to the dances.

Old Quork's Day

Old-time watermen of Ocracoke used to have an old superstition about March 16 and they refused to go out on the water on that day.

Legend has it that if a seaman takes his boat out on March 16 he is likely to meet the same fate as "mean old Tom Quork." According to the old story, it seems long ago a West Indian half-breed was cast away on Ocracoke when his sailing ship was wrecked in a hurricane. The islanders began to call him Tom Quork because his Spanish name was hard to pronounce and his raspy voice sounded like that of the night heron, which the locals called "quorks." From the time he arrived on the island he was considered a mean and wicked man. He lived alone, was unclean, never went to church and spent his days digging clams and fishing. One March day with storm clouds brewing, Tom Quork refused to heed the advice of his fellow fishermen to stay in port and cursed God for the storms He may create and sailed off into the sound. Later the fishermen on the shore saw a waterspout form, move toward and hit Quork's boat. The fishermen got in their boats to help him but his body was never found. From that day forward, March 16 has been known as "Old Quork's Day," a day of traditional sudden storms and a day to remain in port.

Marriage Comfort Blanket

The New Bern newspaper in July 1883 reported that there died in Contentnea Neck, Craven County, a man named Asa Martin, who had been married nine times and each time in the same suit.

Boiling Wells

In January 1897, there was a peculiar report about wells in Beaver Dam Township, Pitt County. It seemed that since the previous snow in December, three wells in the same vicinity had gone to boiling. It was said that the bottom of the wells boiled and bubbled like a pot and there was a strange singing noise that could be heard some distance from the wells. The boiling had no effect on the temperature and the water remained clear and cold.

Look Out for Lizards

During the Civil War the Southern Army drew heavily on the North Carolina farmers for their surplus grain. It became necessary for the state to prohibit the distilling of this crop into spirits. The law was a hard blow to those farmers who had always used their surplus grain to make "arduous spirits" and liked to have some on hand. Petitions poured into the office of Governor Zeb Vance asking him to modify the law so as to allow them to make a few gallons. Among the many excuses offered, the most popular one was that all signs pointed to a good year for snakes and everyone knew it was absolutely necessary to have a few gallons of "spirits" on hand for snake bites.

Marble Sidewalks

Sidewalks of marble in most communities would seem an outlandish extravagance, but not in Marble, North Carolina. The town lies in the immense marble deposits of Cherokee County and since it could be obtained easily, the town board enacted a law in 1933 to use marble for its sidewalks.

North Carolina's Sea Monster

There have been numerous tales and reports of sea monsters up and down the eastern seaboard from Boston to Beaufort, South Carolina, since 1816. Old fishermen and ship pilots around Hatteras and Masonboro had long reported seeing a sea serpent coming and going out of the inlets. Because of the regularity of the sightings, one might believe that there were several sea creatures or possibly that only one sea serpent spent part of his time in Pamlico Sound and the other down on Masonboro Sound on the Cape Fear. An early encounter happened in September 1875, when a party of five gentlemen started from Masonboro Inlet in a small yacht to sail around to New Inlet for the purpose of bringing the boat to Wilmington. The party had sailed before a fine northeasterly breeze for some ten minutes when the wind completely died out and the yacht was left becalmed. While the boat was sitting there, the helmsman observed what he thought was a school of porpoises rolling and playing leisurely toward the yacht. He called his companions, who were asleep below deck, to observe the sight.

They all got up, and for some time the party was at a loss to account for a large black mass of life that was slowly moving toward them. As the mass approached their fears were aroused upon discovering that the black mass was a living serpent at least ninety feet in length. The men scrambled to get to their oars and pulled the boat ashore through the breakers. As the serpent neared the shore he raised his head nearly forty feet in the air, fell back into the water and put to sea at a high rate of speed. A few days later the monster was seen going into Masonboro Inlet. Again the sea serpent created a sensation when he attacked the seine fishery at Masonboro. The seine fishermen were hauling in their large nets of fish when suddenly the sea serpent ran up on one of the shoals and began trying to get the fish caught in the nets. Several of the men tried to attack the beast while one man went to get his gun.

The sea serpent raised his head up, opened his mouth and as the cavity was said to be large enough to swallow a man, the fishermen beat a hasty retreat on the shore. A shot was fired at him without success and as soon as the gun discharged, he beat the water furiously with his tail and put to sea at a remarkable speed. The beast was described as having a body as large as a hogshead, a long neck with curly hair and a head like a horse. It came up on the shoal on large appendage-like fins and was as long as ninety feet. In the 1880s there were numerous sightings of the sea serpent from Cape Lookout to the Pamlico Sound. In September 1883 State Commissioner S.G. Worth was at Cape Lookout with a crew of fishermen trying to collect specimens of North Carolina fish for an exhibit. To their astonishment, they encountered the sea serpent and tried to catch it in their nets but failed. Mr. Worth described it as being immense and about ninety feet long. In the 1890s, fishermen and passengers on steamboats witnessed the sea serpent almost every week. It seemed he liked to stay in the waters around the Pungo River and the Oregon community of Beaufort County. The superstitious folk around North Creek declared the beast a "seven-headed devil" and declared it to be tremendous in size and villainous looking. The fishermen of the Oregon community said it came on shore at night and had "phosphoric eyes." The sea serpent was seen by people on ships going in and out of Hatteras Inlet for the next thirty years. The North Carolina sea monster, or a different one, appears to have come to an untimely end in 1947. In December 1947, the following *Associated Press* article appeared in newspapers nationwide. It was written by the captain of the SS *Santa Clara* and radioed to New York following the ship's report to the Coast Guard that it had "struck a sea monster" off the North Carolina coast.

On Dec. 30, 1947, the Grace Line steamer, Santa Clara, *was cleaving through sunlit calm blue seas, 118 miles due east of Cape Lookout, en route from New York to Cartagena. The* Santa Clara *had just crossed the Gulf Stream when the chief mate, third mate and the navigating officer assembled on the starboard wing of the bridge to take the noon sight at 11:55 a.m. Suddenly the third mate saw a snake-like head rear out of the sea about 30 ft. off the starboard bow of the ship. His exclamation of amazement directed the attention of the other two mates to the sea monster, and as they watched it unbelievingly, it moved in a moment's time, it came abeam of the bridge where they stood and was then left astern. The creature's head appeared to be about two and a half feet across, two feet thick and five feet long. The cylindrically shaped body was about three feet thick and the neck was about one and a half feet in diameter. As the monster came abeam of the bridge it was observed that the water around the monster over an area of 30 or 40 feet square was stained red. The visible part of the body was about 35 feet long. It was assumed that the color of the water was due to the creature's blood and that the stern of the ship had cut the monster in two, but since there was no observer on the other side of the vessel there was no way of estimating what length of body might have been left on the other side. From the time the monster was first sighted until it disappeared in the distance, it was thrashing about as though in agony. The monster's skin was dark brown, slick and smooth. There were no fins, hair or protuberances on the head, neck or visible parts of the body.*

The Mystery of the Gold Button

One winter, about the year 1881, Mrs. Dan Barnett, while walking along the dunes, found a gold button or insignia medallion in an old graveyard that had blown out after a storm on Hatteras Banks. Sometime later, Captain Robley D. Evans, who later became famous as "Fighting Bob," an admiral in the U.S. Navy, came through on his inspection of the lighthouses along the coast. On a visit to Cape Hatteras he saw this button in the home of Mrs. Barnett and it excited his curiosity. Mrs. Barnett told him the story of finding the button, whereupon Captain Evans asked for the button, which was presented to him. About six months later Captain Evans, with a party of strangers, arrived at the Barnett home and asked to be shown the spot where the button was found. Upon discovering the spot, they examined the ground and unearthed the bones of what proved to their satisfaction to be an English admiral, long lost to his people. The party carried the bones away and left old Mrs. Barnett the proud possessor of a gift of fifty gold dollars. Who was this English admiral and what became of his remains?

The Big Freeze of 1940

During the big freeze of January 1940, boats all along the eastern seaboard were ice-bound for the first time since the freeze of 1917–18. The Newport River in Carteret County and numerous other creeks were reported to be frozen over. Boats were reported to be shoving mighty masses of ice ahead of them as they passed down the Inland Waterway. Several large icebergs as large as a small island and extending six feet or more above the water were reported floating in the ocean off Salter Path. Ice floes in Bogue Sound jammed up at the Atlantic Beach Bridge, which offered an ideal landing place for hundreds of gulls who were eating the frozen fish.

Married His First Love

In July 1887 there was a marriage in Kinston between John S. Ware, a leading merchant of Barnesville, Georgia, and Mrs. Barbara Koonce. The marriage of this couple marked the end of a romantic courtship that was cut off by the Civil War. It seems when Sherman's army captured Atlanta there were several small groups of Confederates isolated from their commands. The officers gave them their furloughs until such time as they could get together again. Among those cut off was John S. Ware, who went to Richlands, Onslow County, where he had some friends. While there, Ware became enamored with a beautiful young lady named Miss Barbara Brock. She refused to marry him then, but declared that if he would rejoin the Confederate army she would become his wife at the close of the war. Ware left and rejoined the army, but fate sent him to Georgia and he forgot his first love. He eventually married a young lady from Barnesville and settled there. In early 1887, his wife died and a lady in Atlanta who knew of the North Carolina romance saw her death notice in the newspaper. She mailed it at once to Mrs. Barbara Koonce, the Miss Brock of former days, whose husband had also recently died. Mrs. Koonce wrote a letter of condolence to her old-time love, and the result was the renewal of their former arrangement. Each party had a family of three, all of whom lived under one roof in Barnesville.

First Black Lady Lawyer

In August 1932, the North Carolina Supreme Court licensed the first black female lawyer to practice in the state. She was Ruth Whitehead Whaley of Goldsboro, licensed by the county from New York State.

Father of Thirty-one Children

In June 1927, Fielding Hunt, fifty-nine, married his third bride, Lilla Peyton, thirty-six, in the Pitt County Register of Deeds Office. He was the father of thirty-one children and his "June bride" was a brave soul.

New Bern Relics

April 30, 1893, was the centennial anniversary of George Washington's first inauguration as president of the United States. On that day a bell was cast in Troy, New York, known as the Columbia Liberty Bell. Relics from all over the country furnished the metal for the bell. Among the relics sent from New Bern were fragments of the bell of the old Episcopal Church, copper coins from the reign of George III found in the Episcopal churchyard and the front door bell of the old State Bank. The bell, though cast in Troy, had the metal run into the mold from an electric button pushed in Washington, D.C., by Mrs. Grover Cleveland.

Big Daddy

In July 1873 it was reported that a man in Burke County named Clem Farr, eighty-nine years old, was the father of 39 children and had 102 living grandchildren. He was a true Democrat, and during the Civil War Kirk hanged him. His friends, supposing him dead, were in the act of interring the body when evidences of life were discovered and he was resuscitated. At age eighty-five, he climbed a Seymour and Blair flagpole, ninety feet high, and at the top drank to the health of the Democratic candidates.

Remains of Giants

In September 1871 workmen were engaged in opening a way for the projected railroad between Weldon and Garysburg when they discovered a catacomb mound of skeletons in a bank along the river. The remains, supposed to be Indian, were remarkable in their size. The skulls were nearly an inch in thickness; the teeth were filed sharp and were as large as horses', with perfectly preserved enamel. The bones were unusually long, the femurs being as long as the entire leg of an ordinary man, making them as great as eight or nine feet in stature. Near the skulls were found sharp stone arrowheads, stone mortars and pipe bowls made of soapstone. The bodies were found closely packed together, laid tier on tier as it seemed. One of the skeletons was taken to Petersburg, Virginia, and was presented to an officer of the Petersburg Railroad. The mound was destroyed to make way for the railroad.

Phantom Fleet off Hatteras

In March 1894 the steamship *El Norte* was on its passage from New Orleans to New York. Up to the time she reached Cape Hatteras there was nothing unusual in her voyage. Chief Officer Benson was not in the habit of seeing strange things, but according to his report he witnessed something he had never seen before. He said that on March 18 the vessel was skirting Cape Hatteras, with a glassy swell running from the northwest. There was no wind, and a thin haze stretched along the horizon. That was just about sunrise. The sun had hardly risen above the sea line before Officer Benson had his attention called to a strange spectacle in the west. There was a long, low-lying bank of fog, and over this vapory sea was sailing a shadowy phantom fleet. The hulls of some of the ships were closely outlined, every spar and sail showing distinctly. Mr. Benson said he realized that it was a mirage that he was looking at, but the most important part of the illusion was the fact that every vessel was right side up. A well-regulated mirage at sea generally reproduces images upside down. Officer Benson said he counted twenty-eight schooners, and none of them were in an abnormal position. For two hours, Mr. Benson said, the weird fleet wheeled and circled above the fog bank, and then the sun dispersed the vapor and the ghostly fleet faded.

Real Daughter of the War of 1812

In March 1954, the only real daughter of the War of 1812 in North Carolina, Mrs. G.S. Thomas of Rocky Mount, celebrated her eighty-sixth birthday. Mrs. Thomas had lived her entire life in Edgecombe County, where she and her late husband celebrated their sixtieth wedding anniversary on December 30, 1945. Her father, the late Jesse Mears, was a veteran of the War of 1812. Statistics of the society of the Daughters of the War of 1812, of which she was a member, revealed she was the sole surviving "real daughter" in North Carolina, there being only nineteen left in the United States.

Pot of Gold

In late March 1896, while working in a field near Columbia, North Carolina, Charles Hill, a poor black man, unearthed a tin container full of gold and silver coins. The money was supposed to have been buried by an old miser named Uriah Spruill many years before. The find caused a lot of excitement in the area and digging prevailed throughout the county.

Stumpy Point Snuff War

In 1949 there was an unusual story told about the village of Stumpy Point. It seems that after World War I, this isolated village fervently supported their church and school. Pharoah Meekins was the Sunday school superintendent then and he disliked snuff and tobacco. Being a total abstainer himself, he had very little patience with the habit. One Sunday at the closing exercises of Sunday school, Meekins brought the matter before the congregation. Every user of snuff and tobacco was asked to sign a pledge to stop the habit. Merchants were asked to stop selling tobacco of any form in their stores. Fervor mounted high, and the superintendent was gratified to see that his people were with him on the issue. But there were quite a few who were not in sympathy with him. They were the women snuff "dippers" who would not sign the pledge and who on Monday morning found their snuffboxes empty. It seems they were caught short, because it was on Mondays that they always bought their week's supply. Marching to town like so many "Carry Nations," they descended on the town merchants en masse and demanded that they sell them snuff. Every merchant they went to refused. One irate woman dipper lambasted the last merchant in a tirade of foul language. It so happened that this merchant was a dipper himself and had his package of snuff sitting on the shelf behind him. Pretending he was going to offer the woman a dip, he quickly flashed it before her and then filled his own jaw and placed the package back on the shelf. He again refused to sell a package to any of the crowd of snuff-starved women. A frustrated woman is a dangerous animal and old-timers who recall the incident state that there was a sore bunch of womenfolk in the village. Over threats of no cooking and cleaning, one brave merchant, Wellington Payne, who had not signed the pledge decided to do something. He boarded his shad boat and went to Manteo, where he purchased a good supply of tobacco and snuff. On his return his trade was brisk and he did a thriving business. As time rolled by the other merchants felt the pinch in business and they eased back to stocking their shelves with Rooster High Toast and High Society. And so tobacco and snuff stayed put and the village snuff dippers were happy again.

Just Another Wedding

On a Saturday night in early July 1888, there occurred an unusual marriage in Elmwood, Bertie County. It seems after a normal wedding at the bride's parents' house there was a nice supper with wines, liquors, rye cake, corn cake, common whisky, gin, blackberry pies, etc. Suddenly in the midst of the supper, the wedding party fell to fighting and used pistols, knives, razors, black jacks, bedsteads, andirons, spiders, frying pans and anything they could get their hands on. Many were wounded, but none seriously. They ruined their hats and tore their clothes, but made up and continued to dance all night.

Treasure in Stanly County

In March 1895, there lived a young man named George Sides, the son of Purity Sides and brother of Possum Sides, all of who lived just beyond the Cabarrus and Stanly County line. One day George went down to the section near New London, on the Yadkin Railroad, and began to prospect for gold. There was no problem then to pick up a good day's work at prospecting either in Cabarrus or Stanly County. While prospecting, George spotted a rock that seemed to have been placed there by hand. He turned it over and found another rock. Digging around it, he turned the next one over only to find another rock. After much trouble he removed the third rock. There he found a decayed wooden box containing $4,800 in gold coins. The treasure was believed to be hidden during the Civil War by someone who later died or could not find his hidden cache again.

Monster Shark

In early June 1888, Captain Lorenzo Willis, with two boat crews, killed a large shark in the ocean off Wreck Point near Beaufort. The monster was killed after a desperate fight lasting two hours. When he was first struck with the harpoon he jumped his full length out of the water. After being killed he was towed back to Beaufort. Once he was brought ashore, he was measured and dissected. He was eighteen feet long, eight feet across his breast and weighed two tons. Upon cutting him open, his stomach was found to contain six sharks, the smallest measuring six feet in length. This ugly monster had three rows of teeth, one inch wide and two inches long. The oldest fishermen in the area pronounced him to be the largest shark ever killed on our coast.

Six-toed Marines

In January 1945 there was a report that the quartermaster department at the Marine Corps Air Station, Cherry Point, was in a bit of a quandary, all on account of a Marine with six toes on one foot. The regular GI shoes didn't fit him and facilities weren't available to keep him in custom-made shoes. Notified of the dilemma, Washington suggested the Marine be given a discharge. This was supposedly a regular problem in the military across the country. Just how many six-toed people are out there, anyway?

"Now, Say Tar Heel!"

During the Civil War, the Confederate soldiers were very much in the habit of poking fun at each other, particularly when they happened to hail from different states. The North Carolina troops were particularly sensitive about being called "tar heels," an allusion to the principal product of their native state. One summer day in 1864, a North Carolina regiment had to pass by the camp of a Virginia brigade, and the usual sharp-shooting fire of wit was kept up until they had passed. The last man was several hundred yards behind the regiment. He was a tall, dark, longhaired specimen of the cracker ranger style of soldier, and was riding a pony that was as lean as him. One of the Virginians put the usual question: "What regiment do youens belong to?" "Fourteenth North Caroliny, and now, say 'tar heel!'" responded the soldier, simultaneously bringing his gun to bear on the person of the questioner. The Virginian may have said "tar heel" at some later period of the war, but until the specter from North Carolina was out of range, the inquisitive Virginian preferred to maintain a dignified and impressive silence.

Unnatural Bridge

In the 1880s, near the clay deposit on Fishing Creek was once located the famous ninety-foot whalebone that spanned the creek from the Nash to the Halifax County side. Tradition says that years ago Indians used it in summer to cross, thinking it a moss-covered log. As a matter of fact, it could only be clearly seen in dry weather, or when the water was low. The late Major J.M. Mayo succeeded in digging up from the Nash County bank one half of the lower maxillary-jawbone, but it was so decomposed that it crumbled before it could be handled and moved. Later Professor Kerr took one of the vertebrae to the State Museum in Raleigh, where it could be viewed.

Snake Tale

In 1884, Jonathan Havens of Washington told a story from when he was the captain of the steamboat *Wilson* on the Tar River in the late 1850s. It seems that one day when the steamboat *Wilson* had reached Boyd's Ferry, Pitt County, the steamer received quite a jar on its starboard side. The exclamation, "Heavens, what a snake!" from the cook brought all ship hands on deck. Captain Havens seized his navy gun and, after three well-aimed and effective shots, killed a huge moccasin that measured twelve feet long and was the size of a stovepipe. Lawyer Satterthwaite said then that the snake had been seen often, and that by tradition it had been known on that part of the river for over one hundred years.

Mill Pond Treasures

Back in 1898, E.A. Crudup invited a number of his friends to be present at the draining of his pond near Louisburg. Large crowds of folks were present at the big event. There were the expected abundance of fish for the people to eat and it was said that every person had their fill, but other unexpected curiosities awaited the crowd. One such curiosity that had historical significance was a 162-year-old cannon suspected of being dropped in the pond when the "Spanish last invaded this country." The second surprise came when a turtle weighting 354 pounds was spotted. It was so enormous that it took a team of oxen to pull it from the muck to the bank. The pond also contained several one-eyed catfish. Reliable eyewitnesses vouched for all of the wonderful treasures found in the pond.

Golden Goose

It was reported in February of 1898 that Mr. James E. Burke of Pittsboro owned a goose that was hatched in 1860 and had therefore been on this earth for almost thirty-eight years. During that time, the goose had managed to bring into this world another 225 goslings and at that time had not yet quit reproducing. As might be expected, the old goose had become a great pet to the Burke family. In the summertime when a thunderstorm approached, the old goose would bring her goslings up to the house for shelter.

Agitated Preacher

One Sunday morning in the summer of 1897, the congregation of Union Grove church in the Goose Creek Township near Monroe was much larger than usual, so it was decided to move the service outside in the grove since they all could not fit inside the church. The Reverend Brock, who was conducting the services that warm summer morning, made the mistake of taking his stand to preach near the nest of some yellow jackets. The service had not been going on long when the angry swarm came upon him and began to sting the poor man. He fought the infuriated insects off as best he could then cried out to the congregation, "Brethren, fight 'em off; I came here to fight the devil, and you must fight the yellow jackets!"

Small Wedding

In 1883 in Kentucky, among the presence of a large crowd of curious onlookers at the Buckingham Theater, a Russian dwarf named John Zmaris, age thirty-three and standing forty-two inches tall, was married to a Miss Maria Nail from North Carolina, age thirty-five and standing thirty-one inches tall. Judge Hoke directed the ceremony. Miss Nail was a well-known curiosity around Raleigh.

Antebellum Egg Incident

It seems that before the Civil War, Billie Johnson of Wilson County set out one day for Wilmington. He had with him a basket containing thirteen dozen eggs. Before he reached his destination, the eggs were somehow broken and rendered unfit for market. He thought it would be a pity to waste the eggs, so he stopped by the roadside and an older lady agreed to cook them for him. The story goes that he ate every one of the thirteen dozen eggs and sopped out the frying pan at the conclusion.

Hoover Carts

There are probably very few people now living in eastern North Carolina who have ever seen or heard of the contraption of the Depression days. The Hoover cart, named for President Herbert Hoover, came into being during the depths of the Depression when the agricultural East found itself living from hand to mouth. As Hoover had promised, the cars were in every garage; but it was because the owners could not come up with the money for license plates, taxes and gasoline. In desperation, the front or rear wheels were taken off the automobiles, a cart built on top of the wheels and a mule hitched up to it to provide the power. The Hoover cart became quite a local sensation. The drivers would swing into a struggling service station, request free air for the tires of the cart, a free bucket of water for the mule and drive on. The Hoover cart became a symbol of the Depression in the East. When Roosevelt's campaign began in 1932, the Hoover cart became the standard that eastern farms rallied to return the state to the Democrats. During the campaign there were big Hoover cart parades in many of the small towns. With the return to prosperity the Hoover cart faded from the scene.

The Coddle Creek Hermit

In May 1895 Mr. J.W. Mehaffey of Concord, while on a survey trip on Coddle Creek in the Rocky River section of Cabarrus County, discovered a bona fide hermit. His name was J.P. Langley, aged seventy-five years, who had came from Yadkin County and for years past had lived alone in a hut. The hut, made of poles covered with turf and leaves, had an opening in one side that served as a door. He was known by the locals as a root or herb doctor. He never bought meat; his gun and fishing rod kept him supplied in that line. He was quite an angler and knew all the best fishing holes in Rocky River and Coddle Creek.

Found Like Moses

In April 1874, while the captain and hands of the steamboat *Cotton Plant*, which plied between Tarboro and Washington, were on their return trip down the Tar River, they observed a small coffin floating downstream. Prompted by curiosity, they lowered a small boat and retrieved the coffin and placed it onboard the steamer. Upon opening the lid, inside was found a beautiful newborn baby with an India rubber nipple in its mouth, vigorously nursing from a bottle of milk. It was taken to Washington and placed under the affectionate care of a good old woman.

Interesting Relic

In 1883 Thomas Allen of South Creek, Beaufort County, owned a piece of silk cloth said to be the first ever made in North Carolina. It was a scrap from the silk used to make a vest that was presented to Henry Clay at the Whig convention in Raleigh in 1849. A piece of paper around the scrap bore the signature of the great Whig orator. The scrap was presented to Mr. D. Murphy, father-in-law of Mr. Allen.

Buried Alive

A distressing revelation occurred in March 1896 when, in the company of relatives, the remains of Charles Wooten of Centreville, Pitt County, were disinterred to be placed elsewhere. Having been dead for nearly five years, the box and coffin were found in a good state of preservation, but the side of the coffin was found to have been forced off and the screws broken and Mr. Wooten's body, instead of being on its back, was facing the broken side of the coffin.

Silver Dippers

Silver dippers, not to be confused with silver ladles, were once prized possessions in North Carolina homes, but are now rare antiques. There is an old Scottish custom in North Carolina of owning family "funeral dippers." It seems that according to custom, three full days and three full nights were required between death and the funeral. On the morning of the funeral, a bucket of "spirits" was passed among the men and it was then the special funeral dipper was used.

Healthy Old Chap

In January 1873 there was a man in Alamance County who was seventy-nine years old and had outlived four wives. His numerous descendants were: eight daughters and one son; seventy-three grandchildren; four hundred great-grandchildren; fifty great-great-grandchildren; fifteen great-great-great-grandchildren; and sixty great-great-great-great-grandchildren. It was believed he would marry again.

Old-time Justice

In the New Bern District Superior Court in May 1789, Bradberry Teel of Pitt County was brought before the court for passing counterfeit money. He was brought to the bar and was asked by the court if he had anything to say about why the sentence of law should not be inflicted on him. He said nothing and the court passed the following sentence: He was to stand in the pillory for one hour, have one of his ears cut off, receive thirty-nine lashes on his bare back, remain in jail without bail for two months and forfeit half of his property to the state.

Indian Mound Opened

In the spring of 1883 several government scientists were doing archaeological digs in Indian mounds along the Yadkin River near

Lenoir, North Carolina. In one mound the skeletons of about twenty-seven Indians were found. Of that number, stone surrounded eight and no relics of any sort were found. There were six sepulchers, two of them containing several skeletons lying on top of the other with the bottom one having its arms and legs stretched out and weighted with heavy stones. Over one of the stone graves was found half of one of the mysterious "pitted stones." The pitted stones were oval in shape and had in their center a circular depression large enough to hold a hen egg. At a distance from these stone sepulchers were found nine bodies buried separately and ten others buried in a bunch. Of these ten, one wore ornaments and he was lying at the bottom, face downward and arms outstretched. Around his wrists and neck were beads of seashells alternating with hollow stems of beaten copper plate, about an inch long. His face rested in a large shell about as large as a breakfast plate, of which the whole concave surface was etched with hieroglyphics. The etched figures were mostly square, circular and triangular, though several figures resembled trees and a bended arm. No tracing of animals were found on it. Three other hieroglyphic shells were also found. The presence of the shell beads and conchs indicated the mountain Indians traded with the coastal tribes.

Hawk Killer

In July 1896, it was reported that Hardy H. Draughn of Sampson County had killed 189 hawks during the past thirty-one days. It was said he used some kind of a rubber pipe as a birdcall. The poultry farmers of that section hailed him as a hero.

Interesting Tombstone

Visitors to Elmwood Cemetery in Charlotte may have noticed the unusual tombstone located in the part formerly belonging to St. Peter's Catholic Church. The stone is a marble shaft about six feet high on which is carved an elephant and the following inscription: "Erected by the members of John Robinson's circus in memory of John King, killed at Charlotte, N.C., September 27th, 1880, by the elephant 'Chief.' May his soul rest in peace." The monument remembers an incident when the renowned John Robinson's Circus came to Charlotte. It seems while John King, the animal trainer, was trying to get the elephants out of the train car, Chief, the largest elephant, became enraged and crushed him against the train car. Wild confusion ensued as spectators scattered and the elephant ran up the railroad tracks. Because the mad elephant was loose on the streets, crowds formed and others tried to get a posse formed to shoot it. In the midst of the bedlam, circus workers took Mary, the female elephant, and Boy, another elephant, to go after Chief. The circus workers and elephants met up with Chief at Fifth Street and after a chase on Tryon Street all three elephants were secured by chains with much difficulty at Church Street. All three elephants where driven down Tryon Street back the way they came by an enormous crowd. As the elephants moved along they made a run for the water pump at the Market House. Somehow the elephants got tangled in their chains as they tried to get water at the pump, which again enraged Chief. The crowd made a confused retreat as others with pitchforks and various goads slowly got the elephants back to the circus tents and safely secured. The next day a curious spectacle was afforded by the funeral cortege of John King when his magnificent casket was in a hearse pulled by four handsome white horses followed by the two elephants Mary and Boy.

Is There Elves in Them Thar Woods?

In the woods near the town of Aurora Mr. McCaffity, a hunter, was hoping to scare up some game near Baylies Creek. He was close to the home of Mr. S.G. Watson when he came upon a large hollow cypress tree. What used to be a small doorway was now practically closed together from the growth of the tree. The small door consisted of a board hung by leather hinges and all the work inside looked to be that of a child. He was only able to put his head in the opening to look inside. As he looked inside he could see evidence of human habitation inside the giant cypress. Dumbfounded by his discovery, McCaffity went back to town to share his discovery with others. He brought back several men with him to view the creative abode. The men saw the small hole cut in the tree and knew that only a boy no older than ten could enter through the opening. They peered in the hole again to see a little fireplace made of brick and a chimney made of two joints of stove pipe that ran upon the inside of a hollow crack above. There was also a small bake pan about the size of a large toy stove pan, some little shelves, a tin cup for boiling sweet potatoes and several gourds with small holes cut in the sides and filled with nicely cleaned birds salted and in a good state of

preservation. There inside the tree were also found some pieces of squirrel salted away, a little bag of dried apples and some peanuts. The walls were covered with newspapers. One of the newspapers was the *New York Weekly Mail and Express*, dated March 23, 1887. No one at that time could solve the mystery, though some thought it was the work of a small boy.

An Eagle, a Dog and a Flock of Geese

The following article appeared in an Elizabeth City newspaper in 1880.

On Friday, at Roanoke Island, a soaring eagle, towering in his pride of might, turned his proud eyes from gazing at the sun, upon the quiet yard of Walter Dough, A flock of fat geese that nipped the tender yard grass invited his eye and tempted his taste. The glance was farther to the thought, and down he pounced. The feathers flew, the geese squawked, and there was a sensation in that farmyard—and there was a dog there, too. A goose is put down as a fool, but it is a vulgar error. A goose is a particularly smart fellow. And so was this one the eagle struck in Walter Dough's yard. As soon as he was struck, the goose ran under the house (which was some feet above ground) with the eagle fastened to her back, and the rest of the flock in hot pursuit. And there the fight grew fast and furious. Forty biting and flopping geese on one side, and the king of birds on the other. Although out numbered the eagle maintained the fight and clung to his victim. But soon another enemy presented himself. An enemy more terrible than an army of geese—a bull terrier dog—little, but full of fight. It wasn't fair and the dog had no natural, belligerent rights in a combat between birds, but he came with a bound, and the eagle had no time to settle questions of military ethics; so he threw himself on his back (eagle fashion) to do his best in this hard fight between tooth and toenail. The dog made a lunge at the eagle's breast, and the eagle struck his claws deep into the dog's fore-shoulder. The blows were simultaneous on either side. Both blows told. But a terrier never, and an eagle hardly ever, say die. The only witnesses of the dread combat were the geese who now stood off and looked on; and Miss Martha Brothers, who was singing to her spinning jennie, in the house alone, when the fight began, and who in the end was to be conquering hero, crowned with the laurels of victory. The battle raged. Teeth gnashed. Claws staved. Eyes flashed. But eagles, like men, contend against odds when fighting against fate, and so this eagle's great heart sank within him, and turning tail upon his foe he sought safety in flight. But his retreat was slow and full of difficulty—for he had fifteen pounds of bull terrier swinging behind him. He reached the yard fence. With one desperate effort he sought to scale it. He reached the topmost round. He bore a weight he could not further carry. There they stood, victor and vanquished. Then it was that Miss Martha Brothers, the true hero of the fight, came to the front and won the palm of victory. Seizing a rail, with one fell swoop she came down with a crash upon the eagle's head and left him prostrate, struggling in the agonies of death, the victim of a combination too powerful to be resisted. Alas poor eagle! He measured nine feet between the tips of his outstretched wings.

Romantic Relics

During the centennial celebration at Kings Mountain in October 1880, Mr. William J. Randolph exhibited a romantic relic from the past. The relic was a plain twenty-two-carat gold ring that was found on the Cowpens battlefield in 1821. The inscription read "This and ye giver is yours forever, 1722." The British officer who wore the ring also wore buttons of twenty-carat gold on his uniform and some of the buttons are still owned in the Carolinas. One was presented to General Lafayette in 1826 and others were sent to England, the coat of arms on them revealing the family to whom they belonged.

Ghostly Visitations

There was considerable excitement in Wilmington in the spring of 1885 by what were claimed to be ghostly visitations. An apparition was said to appear at the house of James E. Padrick about eight o'clock every night, and it was believed to be the spirit of Mrs. Carroll, who had died in Bladen County some three years before. The ghost would only appear to the two children of Mrs. Carroll, then living with Mr. Padrick, one aged sixteen and the other eight or nine years old. The spirit only made itself visible to these children, but an audible voice could be heard calling the children at a specific time every night. When the children would enter a certain room, the spirit would throw pillows and other articles around the room, often striking curious witnesses. Sometimes the ghostly presence made itself felt in a room where company was assembled. Mediums were brought in and visitors clamored to witness the event. "She is in your lap, now," remarked one of the mediums to a lady sitting among the visitors in the parlor one night. "Yes, I feel her weight," replied the lady. One night the program was somewhat varied by the appearance of the spirit of a child belonging to another family who died in the same house a year or two before. Night after night curious people gathered at the headquarters of the alleged visitors from the spirit world.

Refused to Die

A startling and sensational episode occurred in Clinton in October 1900. It seems a criminal named Archie Kinsauls was hanged by order of the local court. Kinsauls, after hanging from the scaffold for fourteen minutes, opened his lips and requested to be dropped again. By order of the attending physicians, he was cut down and returned to the top of the scaffold. He was dropped again, which tore loose a wound on his neck from a previous suicide attempt. He was covered with blood from head to toe, and after hanging seven minutes, the doctors pronounced him dead and he was cut down and turned over to his family for burial. It seems when the corpse was taken home, the body was wrapped in wet blankets and resuscitated. Kinsauls was immediately sent by train to Richmond for treatment, where he was listed in good condition.

Shower of Bugs

A gentleman living about three miles south of Raleigh stepped out of his door at daybreak one day in April 1880 and was startled to see the air filled with objects descending gently in showers, like snowflakes. The breeze blew from the east, and he stooped down and saw that they were bugs of a dull gray color, a little smaller than grains of corn. They fell quickly and as soon as they struck the ground began to crawl about in a very sprightly manner. They fell on the house, in the yard, everywhere, a plague of insects. They continued to fall steadily from daybreak until the sun rose. The poultry made a feast of the thousands of bugs before them. The gentleman who observed the phenomenon said that he had known the same thing to occur before, but not for as long.

Historic Quill

In 1876 a man in Lexington had in his possession a quill of a condor that had a history. It was given to Henry Clay in 1824, with an injunction never to cut it until he was elected president, and then he was to write his first message with it. In case he was not elected, the quill was not to be cut until a "Constitutional President wrote a constitutional message for all the States." After Mr. Clay's death, it was given to Millard Fillmore, but he was likewise unable to use it. During the last campaign in 1876 the owner was determined to give it to Horace Greeley should he be elected. The quill, which was uncut, was over three feet long and as large around as a man's thumb.

Cemetery Secrets in Wilmington

The cemeteries of Wilmington have amassed a collection of oddities that have never been forgotten. One such fact began in

1857 when Silas Martin, along with his son John and daughter Nancy, were sailing around the world. Unfortunately Nancy died on the trip. Her father placed her on a chair and submerged her in a cask of liquor. After five months at sea, Silas returned to port and buried his daughter still in the cask of liquor. A simple cross was placed at the grave with the word "Nance" carved upon it. Another grave in Wilmington bears some interesting facts as well. Mrs. Rose O'Neal Greenhow, the famous Confederate spy whose information resulted in victory for the South at Bull Run, is credited with being the only white woman to die in service during the Civil War. Returning from England, where she had been on a diplomatic errand, her vessel was threatened with capture by the federal blockade as it neared Wilmington. She put out for shore in a small boat, which overturned in raging surf, and she drowned. Two days later on September 8, 1864, her body washed up on the shore with a belt of gold coins around her waist. In 1880, W.A. Ellebrook was buried with his Newfoundland dog in his arms. Mr. Ellebrook was a volunteer fireman at the time, and he was trying to save what he could in a fire. He ran into the house and his dog followed to help. However, both never returned from the blaze. The next day the dog's body was found with his teeth sunk in his master's coat and his feet braced in a pulling position against a beam that had pinned the man's body to the floor. The community erected a monument to the two. The monument described Mr. Ellebrook and included an image of the dog on the monument with the words "Faithful Unto Death." There is another story of two gentlemen, Samuel Jocelyn and Alexander Hostler, who in 1810 pledged that the first to die would return in spirit from the other world to visit his friend.

Jocelyn was the first to go after falling from a horse. He was buried two days later. That night Hostler said his companion's voice was heard to say, "Why did you let them bury me alive?" but Hostler dismissed the phantom voices. Two nights later he heard the question again. At the insistence of Hostler the parents of Jocelyn dug up the grave. When the coffin was reached, it was found to be burst open on one side and Jocelyn's body was laying facedown. They had buried him alive. One last story is of Dr. W.W. Wilkins. He was supposed to be the last man killed in the South in a formal duel. The duel that resulted was from political differences with a former friend, Llewellyn Marwick. Marwick disappeared after the episode. Eight years later a skeleton was washed out of a street in the heart of Wilmington after a heavy rain. It was identified as Marwick by his ring, still on the hand of his skeleton. He was apparently murdered and buried under the street.

THE UFO SCARE OF 1947

Sky watching became a new profession in 1947 when UFOs were reportedly seen in forty-three states, the District of Columbia and Canada. The saucers were first reported seen in Washington state on June 25. Then numerous other reports emerged in other western states. The peak came over the July 4 holiday, when they were first reported seen east of the Mississippi. In early July 1947, the first report of a "flying saucer" in North Carolina came when a lady and her son and two neighbors were riding in a car near Asheville shortly before dusk. A very bright object suddenly swung into view and they first believed it was the evening star. After watching it for a few minutes it became much larger and flew lower than a plane normally flies. The four watched as the object swiftly disappeared in the mountains to the west. The next few days had sightings over Greensboro, Raleigh and Wilmington. At Wilmington, five different people reported seeing a "flying disc" at the same time between Wilmington and Carolina Beach. All said it was traveling at a high rate of speed and was unusually bright with an orange tint.

Oysters with False Teeth

In October 1890 an oysterman at New River, Onslow County, found two large oysters firmly attached to a set of false teeth. In 1891 an oyster dredging boat near Morehead City brought up an oyster also with false teeth attached. The oysterman sold them to another man for twenty-four dollars, who in turn sold them to a dentist from Athens, Georgia,

who happened to be attending the Southern Dental Association in Morehead City. The Georgia dentist took his unique purchase to the Dental Association to show off. By sheer coincidence, the dentist who made the teeth was there also, recognized his handiwork and told the story of their loss. It seems Dr. G.K. Bagley of New Bern made the false teeth for a fish dealer in the summer of 1866. The teeth were lost in the fall of the same year when the owner was suffering from an attack of sickness on a boat and they fell overboard. Consequently they had been under the water for twenty-five years. It was said the Smithsonian Institution was seeking to buy the teeth and maybe the curiosity can be found there today.

Long Lost Children Found

In 1910 Mr. James M. Sikes of Columbus County, a veteran of the Mexican War, died at the advanced age of 104 years. Mr. Sikes had been married twice, his last wife being a widow with three children. This second marriage had taken place over forty years before, and Mrs. Sikes had left her children and eventually lost track of them. She had not heard from them during all those years, or even knew where they lived. After her husband's death Mrs. Sikes's heart began to yearn for her children and she employed a man to hunt them up. Following a faint trail and going county to county, the man found one of the old lady's sons and a daughter living in Pamlico. The man told them about the search by their old mother and they gave him photographs of all the children and grandchildren to give to her. Mrs. Sikes was elated over the news and planned that after she got her husband's pension money from the government, she would settle her affairs in Columbus County and make her future home with them.

Babe Ruth's First Home Run

Very few people know that Babe Ruth hit his first home run in a professional game on a baseball diamond in Fayetteville. Babe Ruth learned to play ball on the sandlots of Baltimore, Maryland, and later at St. Mary's Industrial School. Ruth was signed by Jack Dunn on a recommendation by Brother Gilbert of Mount St. Joseph's College and, being a minor, Dunn was made his guardian. At baseball camp in Fayetteville, where the team trained in 1914, Dunn divided his squad into two teams. Ruth was placed on the first team, and although he was signed as a pitcher, was used in his first game as a shortstop. In his initial time at bat, Ruth drove the ball out of the park into a cornfield that adjoined the baseball field. Ruth touched every base and was sitting on the bench before the outfielder even reached the ball. Babe made other long hits during his stay in training camp and later at Oriole Park, but none went so far as his first wallop. In 1916, Dunn sold him to the Boston Red Sox and later he was sold to the New York Yankees and the rest is history.

Strange Death

A sensation occurred near Pelham, Rockingham County, in April 1910. It seems that the four-year-old son of Charles Patterson, a well-known farmer in the area, was nearly buried alive. The boy became ill suddenly and suffered from what appeared to be convulsions, passing into a state of unconsciousness that was mistaken as death. The child was prepared for burial and after being placed in a casket, was taken to Hickory Grove Church to await the funeral services. A number of men and women of the neighborhood remained in the church with the casket for several hours. One woman, prompted by a desire to get a parting look at the child, had the glass pane slipped back from the coffin. The face was observed to be flushed and the body was found to be warm to the touch. Horrified at this distressing discovery, a doctor was hurriedly sent for. The child never regained consciousness and died before the doctor arrived. The incident, however, resulted in the delaying of the funeral for one day longer, to put at ease all doubts that the little one was really dead.

The Tales of Decatur Gillikin

Different localities have their own interesting characters and a few of these "characters" become legendary. Carteret County probably has more than its share, but its most remarkable legend was named Decatur Gillikin. Decatur was a gentle fisherman, six-foot-five-inches tall, who was said to have won more than five hundred fistfights, killed a bear in a wrestling match, stood up to a Union ship in the Civil War and always fought for the poor, regardless of the odds against him. He could not stand anyone laughing at him and he absolutely refused to pay county taxes. According to the stories told,

Decatur Gillikin (born circa 1820) got into his first fight when he was fifteen years old. It seems he went into a saloon in Beaufort to get a cup of yaupon tea and the barkeeper, thinking he wanted alcohol, ridiculed him and said he didn't serve children. Decatur turned to leave and before he reached the door, a group of men began to laugh at him. Angered, he turned around and saw four sailors laughing at his "down east" clothes. He exploded with anger and pounced on the men. When it was all over, Decatur was the only one standing and from then on he was never refused in a saloon again. Sometime later, Decatur signed up on a fast sailing ship for a voyage around the Cape of Good Hope. In the middle of the voyage, it was said that a mutiny occurred and it was Decatur who beat the mutineers into submission. He was amply rewarded and came back to Carteret County and bought a large farm. He got married and settled into a peaceful life. Tired of farming, he eventually built himself a small schooner to continue his livelihood of fishing. Decatur was reckless, if not passionate. Scores of roughnecks thought they were tough and would get Decatur to fight them and he would always come out on top. According to legend, Decatur even killed a trained bear in a wrestling match. It was said he crushed the bear to death when he picked the animal up over his head and slammed him on the ground. This event alone made Decatur the toughest man in the county. On one occasion it is said that Decatur found out that a merchant in Norfolk had cheated a fisherman friend of his. He boarded his boat and sailed to Norfolk and "persuaded" the merchant to even up the account. On another occasion Decatur was in Beaufort and got into a cussing fit. Two ladies overheard the tirade and were greatly insulted. They got up with the sheriff and demanded that he be punished, punishment for cussing in those days being twenty lashes on the bare back at the town's whipping post. The sheriff told the ladies "that punishing Decatur would depend." "Depend on what?" they asked. "Depend on whether or not Decatur wants to be punished," answered the sheriff. When approached by the sheriff, Decatur surrendered himself up to the whipping post, but warned that he better not hear anyone laughing. In an episode during the Civil War, Decatur sailed fearlessly out in his boat, fishing amidst the Union warships blocking the entrance to Beaufort harbor. On his way inshore, a Union warship threatened to fire on him if he didn't surrender up his boat and catch of fish. This so angered Decatur that he told the captain of the warship his name and said that if they fired on him that he would swim over and rip the planks off his ship and tear off his rudder. As the legend goes, the Union captain had heard of Decatur and apologized to him and sailed off. As Decatur got older he continued to farm and fish until his death about 1910. His legend grew and grew and old fishermen say that on the full moon after the first hurricane the ghost of Decatur Gillikin can be seen in his boat entering Beaufort harbor driving schools of mullet inshore for the fishermen to catch.

Hitchhiking Alligator

In July 1931 a man got in his car and began traveling down the river road from Wilmington to Southport. After he crossed the Orton Dam he began to notice something wrong with his automobile. He stopped his car and his eyes about popped out of his head when he found out what the trouble was. A seven-foot alligator had clamped its jaws on the running board and was hanging on like a demon. The reptile was dispatched and weighed two hundred pounds.

Driving in His Sleep

In 1932 a Mr. Hunt of Kinston told several tales of being a somnambulist. He said he had leaped from windows in his sleep, which fortunately were only a few feet off the ground, and once he found himself climbing a rose trellis near his home. While visiting once he decided to take his host's car and do some somnambulist driving. He said he woke up about two miles from the house. Worst of all he said, "I had to wake up the folks in the house to let me in. Thank the Lord, I don't wear a nightgown."

Wheezy Organ Worried Preacher

When things go wrong with some men they vent with a tirade of bad words, but the Reverend Sam B. Stroup of Hickory had other methods: he forgot to preach his Sunday sermon. On a Sunday in April 1932, the organ in the Episcopal church went on a tantrum and as fast as one key would be fixed, another would go haywire and whistles and wheezes were emitted all over the church. The service had just gotten underway and the various noises began to worry Mr. Stroup. Finally he decided he couldn't take anymore and at an opportune time he slipped from the pulpit and crawled to the back of the organ. There he removed his vestments and went to work with a pair of pliers and hammer in all the dirt and grime. Finally a member of the congregation found him and persuaded him to return to the pulpit. Flustered, he hastened on with the service, calling for the offering, and dismissed the congregation. Then the puzzled organist asked, "But aren't you going to preach a sermon today?" Mr. Stroup, abashed, admitted his negligence and then added, "Anyway, I didn't forget the offering."

Large Eagle

In November 1877 Rufus Carson, living near Little Creek, Edgecombe County, killed a gray eagle measuring eight feet from tip to tip. The eagle had destroyed fifteen young pigs and was in possession of two geese when dispatched.

Older than the Nation

In February 1908 there was living in Pine Mill, Texas, at the great age of 132, Mrs. L. Kilcrease. She was believed to be the oldest person in the world. Using the family Bible to corroborate her age, she was born February 10, 1776, in Halifax County, North Carolina. She lived there one hundred years before she went to Texas with her family. Her daughter, aged 98, and her granddaughter, aged 63, lived with her. She enjoyed good health and was able to walk about her house with the use of a cane.

Largest Town in North Carolina

Pantego was without question the biggest town in North Carolina in 1933. In fact, Pantego discovered it was ten times larger than it thought. Pantego, which only had a population of four hundred, contained one hundred square miles of territory, taking in about one-third of Beaufort County. The above-mentioned area is specified in the law passed by the North Carolina legislature incorporating the town. Someone made a mistake; instead of ten square miles, the law incorporating the town reads "one hundred square miles."

Grinning Like a 'Possum

In 1898, state Senator R.H.W. Barker from Lincoln County told a western North Carolina newspaper of an entrepreneur who had 'possums on his mind. G.P. Bowman from Polycarp in Alexander County was such an individual. He was arranging at that time to go into business of raising 'possums for the market. He planned to fence in several acres of woodland using barbwire in such a way as to not allow the 'possums to escape. He also planned to place several hollow logs about the property to give the captive creatures a place to live until they met their fate. And you thought canned 'possum was a big joke.

Fisherman's Luck

In September 1882 it was reported that a poor man named Harris from near Bath, Beaufort County, had found pirate gold. It seems he was wading and crabbing near the shore in the Pamlico River down at Plum Tree Point. He saw something glittering under a stump and reached down in the water and drew up a piece of gold about the size of a twenty-dollar piece. He kept on reaching down and drawing out until he got one hundred pieces. It was believed the gold coins were buried when the stump was on land, since the shore had washed away. Several pieces of broken jar were found and the money was worn smooth with no dates. The find created a local sensation and Harris was offered $1,500 for the gold and the sawmill men around there offered to sell him lumber for some of it.

Could Not Turn the Other Cheek

In the Bailey Township in Nash County back in 1911, two groups of folks just could not see eye to eye. In the heat of an August Friday afternoon, tempers flared. The Sand Level Church was holding a revival that week. That same day, a small distance from the church, a large group of people was enjoying their Friday with a dance and picnic. About the time the church service began, the party had moved into full swing with the whisky and hard cider flowing freely. It was said that the dancing became a nuisance to the revivalers. The parson and his trusted deacons approached the group in hopes of them easing some of the noise and the inappropriate dancing. The parson and his "chosen ones" were told to return to their flock and let the partiers go about their business. A short time later the entire congregation joined their leaders amongst the partiers. A boisterous man from the partiers' side poked his head in the parson's face and asked, "What's that you say parson? You want us to stop dancing, huh? Now just you listen to me parson while I vociferate a little. I want you to hear my bazzoo when it toots. If you and your bunch do not like the way us folks cuts the pidgin wing, you just put wheels under your little church and roll it away. Do you follow me parson?" About that time knives, razors and pistols were brought to hand and the fight was on. The scuffle numbered about seventy-five people. They broke out about four o'clock that afternoon and did not stop until around nine o'clock that night. At the height of the free-for-all, Deputy Sheriff Dan Bissett appeared to try and bring things to an end. However, he was disarmed by the rumblers and "sent back from whence he came."

Family-size Potato

In 1854 near Oxford, Mrs. Martha Taylor grew a sweet potato that weighed ten and three-quarter pounds. The following year she showcased the monster potato at the Henderson Agricultural Fair. She was so proud of the potato that she kept it on her mantel for the next four or five years. During that time the potato grew vines that ran around her clock and up to her ceiling. The potato was sent to the Agricultural Museum in Raleigh in 1880 to be preserved for display. Unfortunately, by that time, the potato weighed less than one pound.

Walking for the Money

In June 1879 it was reported that Miss Mattie Potts, a resident of Philadelphia but a native of Edenton, North Carolina, was on a walking mission. It seems she took a bet for $5,000 that she could walk from Philadelphia to New Orleans, a distance of twelve hundred miles, and return in five months. She was reported as being very attractive, well dressed and walking at a rate of thirty miles a day. She passed through Greensboro in the middle of June.

The Mummy of Laurinburg

For over fifty-four years, the mummified body of Frinnizzee Concippio hung in the funeral home in Laurinburg. Concippio, called "Spaghetti" because his name was so hard to pronounce, was widely known in eastern North Carolina and was visited for years by thousands of schoolchildren and the curious from around the country. The strange tale of Spaghetti began May 3, 1911, at a carnival in McColl, South Carolina, a little town nine miles south of Laurinburg. He was a trumpeter in a circus band and was hit on the head with a tent stake during a bitter argument with another carnival worker over the affections of a woman. Rushed to a Laurinburg hospital, he died a few hours later. His body was turned over to M.J. McDougald's Funeral Home, where it remained. Concippio's father, unable to speak English, came to Laurinburg with an interpreter and paid undertaker John McDougald part of the cost of embalming the body. The father said he would return to arrange for the burial, but in the event he did not get back, "to dispose of the body as you see fit." McDougald held the body, waiting for the father or relatives to claim it, but no one came. Time passed and McDougald's business flourished, and in need of room he had to find someplace to put the dead trumpeter. He placed a heavy cord under the body's arms and hung it on a spike on the embalming room wall. There the corpse stayed, clad only in a loincloth, until it slowly became a mummy. In 1939, the mummy and the tent stake were placed in a sealed glass cabinet when the firm moved to a new location. Just prior to World War II, newspapers and wire services picked up the story about Laurinburg's mummy and the story reached the Italian ambassador in Washington, D.C. Mussolini's representative wrote to McDougald offering him $500 to bury Concippio, who was an Italian national who never became an American citizen. McDougald refused, saying he would take $5,000 to defray embalming and storage fees incurred over the twenty-five-year period. Before the ambassador could receive instructions from Rome, war broke out and the matter was apparently forgotten. The body was used many years later as an exhibit in a court case to prove that an embalmed body can be preserved indefinitely. What became of the mummy after 1965 is unknown.

The Treasure of Pharoah Farrow

According to an old story, there was once a wealthy shipbuilder at Avon on the Outer Banks named Pharoah Farrow. He was a hard man, owned many slaves and his plantation was the marvel of the neighborhood. It was said that he once called a visitor back to his private room and, pointing to a chest, told him to lift it. Having failed to budge it, Farrow raised the lid and it was found to be filled with gold coins. One day when Farrow was older, he called to his side his most faithful slave. He blindfolded the slave and made him transport the hoarded gold to a corner of his estate where, under the cover of darkness, he buried it deeply in the white sands of Kinnekeet. A few days later, old man Pharoah Farrow died in his sleep. The old slave in later years told the tale of how he buried the gold, but none of it was ever found. Fifty years after the death of the old man, a descendant of Pharoah Farrow had his fortune told in New Bern. The gypsy woman told him there was a chest of gold buried in the corner of the barnyard on the plantation where he lived at Avon. Many efforts were made to find the buried money, but the exact spot was never located. Many years later the graves of Pharoah Farrow and his family became broken and crumbled and a baseball diamond covered the site of his once beautiful house. The treasure has yet to be found.

A Race for a Bride

There was a strange story out of Pollocksville in May 1880 concerning a race for a bride. It seems that Moses John Miller and Alexander Bibb, two well-to-do young farmers, were in love with the same girl, Leonora Lloyd. She was not able to decide which she liked the best. On Sunday morning Bibb walked home from church with her and she left him under the impression that she would marry him. The next night Miller went to see her and understood her to say that she would marry him. Both men happened to go to the courthouse the next morning to procure a marriage license. After getting the necessary documents, they met at the courthouse door. After some talk and realizing the predicament they were in, they agreed that the first man who reached her house should marry her. Her residence was about one mile from the courthouse and both men wasted no time starting on the race for the bride. Bibb soon quit the main road and dashed into the woods, expecting to take a shortcut and reach the house first, but Miller kept to the main road and got to the home stretch eight minutes before his rival. The men were in sight of each other going up the lane to the house. Bibb's effort to overtake Miller was superhuman and he overtook Miller only to faint on the porch at the feet of his ladylove from sheer exhaustion. When the situation was explained to her, she concluded to marry Mr. Bibb. Her sympathies were won over by seeing him faint, believing that he who faints at the danger of losing a bride must love her more.

Do You Smell a Rat?

Mr. John Brock of Craven County found himself with a number of burdens in the summer of 1884. He had decided to take on the task of moving some old corn in his corncrib and in doing so uncovered a "five-star rat hotel." Brock said he killed 290 large rats during the move, but that is not the end of it. Later that night Brock heard the cry of his chickens. He went out to see what the ruckus was about. To his dismay, he found one of his young chickens in the claws of a large rat. He attempted to kill the overgrown rodent, but was unsuccessful. He then latched on to the chicken and began a tug of war with the varmint. The rat managed to get away with his prize. Determined not to lose another chicken to the thieving devils, he set some steel traps to catch the rats. Mr. Brock managed to catch one when he went to check his trap after hearing a rat squeal. As he approached the cage to remove the rat about a dozen other large rats surrounded him. The rats closed in on him and sent him running for safety. Mr. Brock had never had to run from rats before, but his experience sent him looking for a better mousetrap.

Old Gander

In 1892 a Sleepy Creek man from the Goldsboro area named C.W. Smith was said to have a gander that had been on this earth for around ninety years. He said that the bird had been full-grown long before the Civil War and that the gander had its wing broken by a gunshot during the war. The goose had gained popularity from an article written about it in a New York newspaper after the Civil War. Mr. Smith believed at that time that the bird was probably reaching the end of its long life because his eyesight and appetite were beginning to fail.

Magnetic Ground

In September 1887 it was reported that at a certain quarter-acre of ground near Asheboro had been struck 140 times by lightning during the past summer.

North Carolina Crystal Ball

In October 1895 a New York City newspaper reported that there was a fine display of crystals and gems going there. The most stunning was a great crystal ball, absolutely pure and flawless, cut from a crystal found in Chestnut Hill Township, Ashe County, North Carolina. The firm of Tiffany cut it, and it was said that it took three hundred hours to make the sphere. Also in the show were rare crystal arrowheads made by North Carolina Indians and ruby sapphires found in Macon County. One of the sapphires was a rare bronze color of great beauty.

Hair Albums

About 1887 there was a craze among the ladies of North Carolina in creating hair albums of men's hair. Young women would besiege their young gentlemen friends for locks and of course they would happily comply, especially when asked by the right damsel. The lock of hair would be tied with a blue ribbon and attached in an album. Over it would be written the name, age, eye color, date of receiving the memento and other personal remarks, which might or might not be complimentary, as the album was never to be seen by any other than feminine eyes.

Black Hero of the Revolution

Very few people know that there was a black man named Ned Griffin of Edgecombe County who served in the Continental army of the Revolution and was rewarded for his services by the gift of freedom and the rights of citizenship and suffrage. In the acts of the North Carolina General Assembly for 1784 is found:

Whereas Ned Griffin, late the property of William Kitchen, of Edgecombe County, was promised the full enjoyments of his liberty, on condition that the said Ned Griffin should faithfully serve as a soldier for and during the term of twelve months; and whereas the said Ned Griffin did faithfully on his part perform the condition, and whereas it is just and reasonable the said Ned Griffin should receive the reward promised for the services which he performed…it is hereby enacted, by the authority of the same, that the said Ned Griffin, late the property of William Kitchen, shall forever hereafter be in every respect declared to be a freeman; and he shall be, and he is here enfranchised and forever delivered from the yoke of slavery; any law, usage or custom to the contrary thereof is anywise notwithstanding.

Punishment for Bigamy

North Carolina used to be tough on anyone indulging in more than one wife. In June 1858 the Cumberland County Superior Court convicted H.C. Bartless of bigamy. He was sentenced to be branded on the left cheek with the letter B, to receive thirty-nine lashes on his bare back, to be imprisoned for thirty days and then be given thirty-nine more lashes before being set free. He had married four wives.

Huge Snakes Galore

In August 1877 it was reported that a huge snake was killed at Beasly Hole near Burgaw. It was described as being of the anaconda species, being about thirty feet in length and larger around than a man's body. When discovered and killed the snake was in the act of swallowing a yearling deer. Later in October 1877, it was reported that a large rattlesnake had been seen in Mitchell County and from the description given it was like the one seen lurking around Newton. The Mitchell snake was spotted, had a yellow head, was about two feet in circumference, about fifteen to twenty feet in length and made a loud bellowing noise when disturbed. A group was organized to dispatch the monster.

Mysterious Walls

There was once an ongoing mystery that captivated the state newspapers back in the 1800s: the discovery of buried walls. As far back as 1780, a wall of rock was discovered underground in Rowan County, which was traced for several miles. In March 1877 it was reported that on the farm of Thomas Glasgow, about two miles from Enfield, there was discovered a solid brick wall under the ground. Most of the bricks were two and a half inches thick, eight inches long and seven and a half wide. The full length of the wall had not been determined at the time, but an ancient-looking sword and axe were found in the ground adjoining the wall. In the 1880s an underground wall was discovered in the vicinity of Asheville and at Chronly, on the Charlotte and Columbia Railroad line. The one at Chronly consisted of walls of a building one hundred feet by sixty feet, built of well-burnt bricks. It was said that the foundation of Hope Mills factory near Fayetteville was partly built of sandstone rock that once formed the "Indian Walls," a solid rock structure found in a creek in the vicinity of the factory.

Civil War Tale

Eastern North Carolina formerly produced all the peanuts grown in the United States and called them "goobers." There is a story of a North Carolina regiment in the Confederate army that was sent into Northern Virginia early in the war. Marching along one day, as hungry as usual, these men came upon a field of clover, something they apparently had never seen before. Mistaking it for peanuts, they broke ranks, leaped the fence and began tearing up the roots of the plants. Their disappointment was bitter and afterward the regiment went by the name of "Goober Grubbers."

End of the Rainbow in Black Jack

Washington Parker of Black Jack, Pitt County, was out digging postholes with his auger for a fence in 1914 when the unexpected happened. The auger struck a large iron object that appeared to be a pot. Mr. Parker dug up the curiosity only to have the chance of a lifetime happen. Once he got the pot to the surface he removed the lid to find gold! Someone had buried the pot some years back with $1,640 face value in gold coins. Folks suspect that someone put it there from the turpentine industry in the area during the Civil War, because of the lack of banks and the fear of being robbed. Whoever buried the loot must have been killed during the war or forgot where they buried it because the gold remained there undisturbed for half a century.

Garbage Gut

In 1903 it was reported by William Johnson of Buie's Creek that a young neighbor of his named Elmon Matthews set out to make a name for himself; or maybe he was just really hungry. The young fellow must have had a stomach made of rubber because what was reported that he ate would discourage even the toughest goat. He was said to have eaten in one setting the following: 1 gallon of mulberries, 1¼ pounds of lard, 1¼ pounds of candy, 1 pound of collards, ½ pound of meat, 1 pound of bread, 4 large biscuits, ½ pint of molasses and 1gallon of lemonade and ½ gallon of water to wash it all down.

Tar River Lives Up to Its Name

When Confederate soldiers evacuated Washington they did not want to leave anything the Yankees could find useful. Among the items disposed of were one thousand barrels of tar and turpentine. The soldiers rolled the barrels down by Taft's store in Pitt County and dumped the contents into the river. A couple months later four hundred Yankee prisoners were steamboated in from Salisbury to be traded for captured Confederate soldiers. The steamboat *Colonel Hill* was tied up at the wharf at Taft's store so that the boys in blue could take a bath in the river. Unfortunately for them, they were bathing where the tar and turpentine had been dumped. It was not long before they were covered from head to toe with the gunk. It was said that they had meat rations in one hand and a stick in the other to scrape the goop from their bodies. One soldier commented, "Darn if we haven't found Tar River at last, the whole bed is covered with pitch."

Hero of the Revolution

There is an old story from New Bern concerning the horrible fate of one of its Revolutionary War soldiers. It seems James Davis established the first printing press in New Bern in 1749 and was the father of three sons: John, Thomas and William Davis. John Davis served in the Revolution and in 1780 he was taken prisoner in Charleston, South Carolina, and was imprisoned on a British man-of-war. It seems that the British captain of the prison ship tried to make the American prisoners do duty on board the ship and John Davis absolutely refused. Davis was then severely whipped, but continued to refuse the captain. The captain then put Davis in a boat and took him to every ship in Charleston Harbor where he was given fifteen lashes at each one. Davis was then returned to the prison ship and told if he would draw a bucket of water from the ship's side they would cease the whipping. He replied, "If his Majesty's whole navy was on fire and that one bucket of water drawn by me would extinguish the flames, I would not draw it." The flogging was then resumed and continued until he died, being wholly or partially disemboweled.

Unusual Convention

A curious incident occurred in Halifax County in 1860 when a meeting was held asking Napoleon III, the French emperor, to take North Carolina under the country's wing. The convention was held on October 14, 1860, at Hill's Ferry, now called Palmyra, about six miles from Scotland Neck. There were about three hundred people in attendance from Halifax, Martin, Edgecombe, Warren and Bertie Counties. It was an all-day meeting with the usual big dinner, barbecue and alcohol. There was a lively discussion over two sets of resolutions that were offered. One resolution was to the effect that North Carolina would go back under the protection of the English government. The other resolution, which was unanimously passed, wanted North Carolina to form an alliance, offensive and defensive, with France under Napoleon III.

Dismal Swamp Monster

In 1901 there were strange tales about a monster in the Dismal Swamp on the North Carolina state line. Weird tales were told of some beast in the swamp with eyes that had a phosphoric glow. Numbers of farm animals were found ripped apart and the general public was scared out of their wits. In April 1902 a hunter killed the monster near Deane, Virginia, while it was devouring a dog. The beast looked more like a wolf than anything else.

Political Interruption

In June 1897 during the midst of a political rally in Richmond, Virginia, the North Carolina delegates marched in late singing "The Old North State." The association was compelled to suspend the business at hand to wait for them to quit marching and singing and take their seats. The head of the rally gave a neat turn to the interruption by saying, "North Carolina is entitled to interrupt any convention at any time, for she was not only among the foremost in the late war, but in the first revolution. A year before Jefferson penned his immortal Declaration of Independence, North Carolina adopted the Mecklenburg Declaration. So I propose three cheers for the 'Old North State.'" These were enthusiastically given and then the head of the rally said, "And now, let North Carolina take her seat and be quiet!!"

A Wedding in the Mountains

In 1884 there was an account giving a detailed description of a wedding in the mountains of North Carolina. The account is very interesting, giving us a picture of life as it was then.

> *The bride was arrayed in a gorgeous calico of the "Dolly Varden" pattern, brilliant with all the colors of the rainbow; each separate color representing some feathered bipeds, from gobblers to peacocks. In her hair was an enormous crown of hollyhock blossoms. Pinned on the top of her head, and extending to her waist was a scarlet ribbon four inches wide. The bridegroom, who was without beard, had on a blue jeans coat of the "clawhammer" or "scissor-tail" style with brass buttons about the size of a silver quarter. He had on butter nut*

colored pants with a red flannel stripes sewn down the seams of the legs; a white flannel vest with eagle buttons, a cotton velvet collar and brogan shoes, greased with lard and tied with coon skin strings. After a short ceremony the whole company retired to the supper. The supper was excellent, consisting of pancakes, maple molasses, gingerbread, hominy, pies, venison and various "spirits." The wedding presents were numerous and were intended for use rather than ornament, as follows: 1 bread tray, 1 dozen iron spoons, sausage grinder, 2 wash tubs, 3 flat irons, 6 brooms, 1 dozen tin cups and pans, 2 stew pots, 2 skillets, and a variety of other articles. There was one gift which the writer could not figure out, a sugar trough with rockers in it.

BIG BABY

In April 1825, it was reported that the wife of Michael Wilder of Chowan County safely delivered a baby daughter weighing $18\sqrt[3]{4}$ pounds. The mother and child were reported as both doing well.

CAR SPEED MUSIC BOX

In August 1914 Frank Osborn of Stella, Carteret County, invented what you might call a car speed alarm. The invention was a small music box, which was attached to an automobile that would play the opening bars of some tune when the car reached a certain speed. It was said that one of the large automobile manufacturers had already agreed to purchase the invention.

Family of Soldiers

In 1896 there were living in Buncombe County eight Stevens brothers who served in the Civil War for four years and came home unharmed. At one time, they were all under the command of Colonel J.E. Ray of Asheville.

Plowed up Gold

In May 1901 Dock Fuller was doing some plowing near the academy in Burlington when he plowed up a vessel containing sixty odd twenty-dollar gold pieces. The cache was supposed to have been buried during the Civil War by the Newbern Bank, which was refugeeing there at the time. The gold pieces, with dates between 1854 and 1858, were covered with dirt, but after washing were found to be in good condition.

Antarctica Peak Named

In the mid 1960s, James G. Sullivan, a native of Ahoskie, was honored for his geological research in the trans-Antarctic mountains of Antarctica. A peak in that region was named "Sullivan Nuntak" in his honor. He spent fifteen months doing research in the area.

Lost Boy Found

In 1865 a little boy, four years old, the son of Mr. and Mrs. Chauncey, was playing on the public road in the suburbs of Washington near his parents' house. He disappeared mysteriously and after much searching and anguish it was concluded that he wandered away to the woods, became lost and had probably been devoured by some wild animal. The only circumstance that created any suspicion was that a tobacco wagon had been seen to pass the road about the time the child was seen last, and the grief-stricken parents clung to the hope that he was still alive. After years of no word, all hope was given up and the matter became one of quiet suffering in the family. In early 1893 a letter was received by the family from a man in Georgia named Chauncey who happened to see the name in a scrap of an old North Carolina newspaper. Remembering that he was from North Carolina, he supposed he might get some information on his parentage by writing. After several letters, he came to Washington and was met at the train depot by his aged parents and was identified by some marks on his body. It seems he was kidnapped by the tobacco wagoners, carried around with them until they reached Georgia, placed in a Catholic hospital there and when he grew up worked in a marble yard. He was thirty-two years old and was happy to get back to his lost life.

Remarkable Marriage

It was in Washington in July 1879 that seventy-year-old W.H. Perry, captain of the government buoy tender *Maggie*, married a Mrs. Hanly, age fifty-six. The remarkable thing about this marriage was how they met. It seems several years before, Mrs. Hanly, who was a widow and accomplished authoress from Ohio, lost her young son to death. She was living in Washington at the time and she buried her son among strangers in the Methodist churchyard there. In May 1879, Captain Perry lost his wife and she was buried near the grave of Mrs. Hanly's son. Soon after her death, he was called away on duty. On leaving he ordered a carpenter to enclose his wife's grave. The carpenter carelessly extended the enclosure over part of the young man's grave. This troubled Mrs. Hanly, but she was a modest woman and a stranger and hesitated doing something about it. On the last day of June, Mrs. Hanly and Captain Perry met by accident for the first time, at the graves of their loved ones. They shook hands; they talked of their troubles and then became fast friends. Their friendship grew quickly, which led to their marriage.

Saved by a Curve

A remarkable incident happened in April 1884 when the passengers traveling on a train on the Chester & Lenoir Narrow Gauge Railroad raced a tornado. The train had passed Lowerysville and was speeding in the direction of Lincolnton when all onboard

were startled by a roaring sound that could be distinctly heard above the noise of the train. The passengers glanced back and saw an immense tornado tearing along the railroad tracks directly behind them. The engineer was one of the first to discover it and he pulled the throttle wide open and the exciting race began. The whirlwind was no more than five hundred yards behind the train and the anxious passengers soon became aware that it was gradually gaining on them. Many of the ladies in the car cried and carried on, while the men danced about the car, vainly yelling at the engineer to put on more steam. The race continued this way for two miles, when the train turned a curve in the tracks. As the tornado struck the curve it left the railroad track, speeding off into the fields. At the time it left the track it was not more than three hundred yards behind the train. It was a thrilling race, and all the passengers blessed that curve from the bottom of their hearts.

North Carolinians in Texas

On March 2, 1836, fifty-seven men signed the Texan Declaration of Independence against Mexico at Washington, Texas, on the Brazos River. Of the signers, nine were North Carolinians: J.B. Badget, age twenty-nine; George W. Smith, age thirty-three; S.C. Robinson, age fifty; Robert Potter, age thirty-six; E.O. Legrand, age thirty-three; William Clark Jr., age seventy-three; William C. Crawford, age thirty-one; John Turner, age thirty-four; and Jesse Grimes, age forty-eight.

The Amazing Life of General William W. Loring

According to a rare sketch of his life, General William W. Loring was born near Goldsboro, Wayne County, in 1823, and moved with his family to Florida at an early age. As a young man he fought in the Indian wars in Florida and at the age of nineteen was a second lieutenant. He then studied law in Virginia and returned to Florida as an attorney and was elected to the state legislature for three years. He entered the U.S. Army in 1846 as a captain. In 1847, he was actively engaged in the Mexican War and rose to major under General Winfield Scott. He led the advance to the city of Tacubaya Causeway, in which one of his arms was carried off by a cannonball. He afterward operated with distinction as colonel in the Indian country of Oregon, and from 1851 to 1856 commanded in the Texas frontier and Mormon territory. In 1859 and 1860, having a leave of absence, Colonel Loring traveled through Europe, Egypt and the Middle East. In 1861, he was ordered to command the Department of Mexico, but resigned immediately upon hearing that Florida had seceded. He was soon after appointed a brigadier general in the Confederate army and ordered to command twenty thousand men in western Virginia. He was again promoted and assigned to command the western division of the Confederate army. In April 1865 he surrendered with General Joseph E. Johnson to Sherman in North Carolina. After the war, Loring engaged in banking in New York City. In 1869, General Loring was asked to accept military service in Egypt and he entered the army of the Khedive. By 1877, General Loring was promoted to commander in chief of the army and was given by the Khedive the decoration known as "Osmahneeyah" or "grand commander," and the decoration known as the "Medijedah," or "grand officer," which was at the time the highest order ever conferred upon a foreigner in Egypt. In 1879, he was mustered out of the Khedive's service and returned to the United States, eventually living in New York City. Loring began writing his experiences, contributing articles to magazines and in 1884 published the book *A Confederate Soldier in Egypt*, which gave an entertaining narrative of his service under the Khedive. He died in New York City in 1886.

Sixty-eight Children

In January 1884 there lived on Crowder's Creek, Gaston County, a former slave named Samuel Johnson. He was born in 1809 near Tuckaseege Ford, Gaston County, on the plantation of Robert Johnson and lived there for many years. Samuel had five wives who had borne to him sixty-eight children.

Giant Pie

In August 1848 there was a public dinner in Goldsboro. About 1,500 people attended the affair. There were barbecued beeves, hogs and lambs and an enormous pie. The pie was composed of 120 chickens and 2 hogs.

Indian Gallows in Bertie County

In the 1830s there was a landmark still standing in Bertie County known as the Indian Gallows. The story goes back to the friendly Tuscarora Indians under King Blount who lived on a reservation in Bertie County. The reservation, given to them in 1748 by the royal government, contained 12,500 acres on the Roanoke River. By 1756, the Tuscaroras decided to leave Bertie County and join their kindred in New York state, as one of the five Indian nations there. From time to time in previous years, they had leased small areas of their reservation to the adjacent white settlers. This increased the many acts of injustice against them by the whites and led to their decision to move. In 1756, the state government ratified and confirmed these leases and confirmed a lease to three men of the residue of the lands for the next 150 years. For a number of years, at rare intervals, the Indians sent agents from New York to Bertie County to collect their rents and look after their holdings. Under legislative authority the tribe was permitted to sell out their interests and the money was paid to them and a deed of release executed. The last recorded time a Tuscarora Indian was in Bertie County was in 1832. Three Indians, Longboard, his wife Saccarusa and their baby, Juno Columbo, appeared in the county, having walked from New York. Supposedly they did not ask directions to the reservation, but walked to "Sapona Town" where the tribe had lived some 70 years before. Near the center of the reservation were two large unusual trees that were a local landmark. These two oak trees, standing about thirty feet apart, had the limb of one tree growing into the other tree about twenty feet off the ground. The locals considered these Siamese trees a natural curiosity. While Longboard and Saccarusa were there, they cut into one of the Siamese trees and found certain marks, which they told curious bystanders recorded the fact that two men and one woman had been hanged on these trees. The trees remained in the forest until one was blown down in a violent storm. The other tree stood for a few years with its limb sticking out like an arm. The tree decayed to the point that the owner of the land cut it down and a set of chairs was made from the wood. Thus passed away the Siamese twins of the forest known as the Indian Gallows.

Horned Snakes

In August 1877 a man from Burnt Chimney, Rutherford County, was in Charlotte exhibiting several snakes; one even had horns. The horns were said to project perpendicularly from the snake's head and were about an inch long. They were brownish in color and tapered from the head. In October 1877 John T. McKay of Fayetteville left at the Agricultural Museum in Raleigh a specimen of venomous snake which they called "Cerastes" or "horned snake." This snake supposedly had a horn one and a half inches in length at the end of its tail and in battling would thrust the horn at its prey with deadly effect.

Crypt in a Boulder

In the Jeffreys family cemetery north of Rolesville is found an unusual grave chiseled into a large boulder. The grave holds the remains of William Andrew Jeffreys (1817–1845), son of Osbourne Jeffreys. William was an attorney and was elected state senator just a year before his death. His father chose the massive boulder for his son's tomb because it could not be moved. William's body was placed in a burial vault and his father went to Raleigh and engaged a stonemason working on the state capitol to take up the project. It took the stonemason nearly a year to complete the crypt. The body was removed from its vault and transferred to the dappled gray boulder. The top of the carved vault was sealed with a six-foot inscribed marble slab.

To Catch a Thief

At one time, Lorenzo Dow, the noted traveling preacher who was probably more famous than the president, stopped often in North Carolina. He was said to be eccentric, have a peculiar mind and have a sense of the dramatic in everything he did. Dow preached in New Bern and proclaimed he would again preach in New Bern, three years in advance, at a prescribed time. On the appointed day, a large crowd assembled at the church to hear him preach, even though Dow had not been seen or heard from. As the exact time Dow was to speak approached and there was still no word from him, many believed that he had missed the appointment and started to leave the church. Suddenly, Dow popped up from behind the pulpit, having concealed himself in the boxed pulpit unnoticed, and began chastising them for "being of little faith." Another story about Lorenzo Dow is how he used a rooster to find a thief. It seems he was giving a tent revival and staying in a hotel in a small town. One day the proprietor, who knew Dow often used very unusual means of leading sinners to repentance, asked Dow to help him find the thief who had stolen the wallet of another guest. Dow agreed to help the hotel manager and told him he would catch the thief. Dow told the manager to get the rooster in the barnyard and the big iron pot in the back yard and bring them into the hotel parlor. He instructed the proprietor to get a small table, turn the pot over and put the rooster underneath it. Next he was to close the shades to dim the light and then call in all the hotel guests. The directions were followed and the puzzled guests were ushered in the parlor. Dow told the audience that someone had stolen a wallet from a guest and the thief may be present. He asked that if the guilty party wanted to be forgiven, this was his opportunity. No one responded and Dow asked them all to get in a line. He told them that there was a rooster under the pot and asked them to touch the pot with the fingers of their right hand as they filed past the table. If the thief was among them the rooster would crow if the thief touched it. The shades were lowered to the point of darkness and the guests were sent past the pot to touch it. Nothing was heard from the rooster as they passed, and everyone was confused. Dow ordered the shades raised and asked everyone to put out their right hand. Dow went down the line and soot appeared on each person's hand except one. Dow announced that he was the thief; his guilty conscience made him fear the rooster.

Large Family

There lived in 1894 a man named Joshua Hudson of Norwood, Stanly County, who was ninety-nine years old. He had been married three times and had 325 living descendants. He had never tasted a drop of medicine in his life.

Beach Vacation

It was reported in 1857 that there was a wealthy plantation owner of Edgecombe County who during the summer would carry his slaves with him to Nag's Head for a month's vacation. It was a peculiar sight to see the caravan of wagons headed for the beach.

Terrapin Hedges

One of the many lost sights along the coast was something called "Terrapin Hedges." One hundred years ago, the capture of sea turtles, or terrapins, was a coastal industry. The coastal fishermen would use wood from shipwrecks and build a line of planks edgewise along the shore for as long as two miles. This wooden hedge would be just above the high-water mark, their ends projecting over boxes sunk in the sand every seventy-five feet. A terrapin would crawl up to the beach to lay its eggs and would follow the hedge until it would fall in the sunken box. They were then transferred from the boxes to an

enclosure projecting in the water, where they were fed and kept until winter and then sent to market in Baltimore and Philadelphia.

Alive and Kicking in 1887

Billy Whitley of Stanly County was 112 years old when a brief biography described him in 1887. He remembered seeing soldiers returning from the Revolutionary War. Mr. Whitley took a wife when he was thirty-three and remained married to her for seventy-five years; she passed away in 1881 at the age of 101. It was said he owned a musket that was used in the fight at Yorktown, Virginia, which he used to kill his fair share of deer. The former owner of the musket heard Washington and Cornwallis's conversation of the surrender. He also possessed his father's pocketbook that must have been 125 to 150 years old. He said that he was on his third set of teeth, but they were his own, not false teeth. He had cut his own firewood and farmed fourteen acres of land the previous year. He had been a member of the Old School Baptist Church for over sixty years at that time. He was also said to have never had a lawsuit against him, told a lie or had to pay a doctor's bill. His extraordinary age was reported again three years later in 1890.

Spanish Coins

In September 1859 a slave boy found a Spanish doubloon on the lands of Simon Gay in Nash County. It was first believed to be nothing but an old brass button. In May 1903 Charles Game was digging up an old stump on the lands of John Game in Boon Hill Township, Johnston County, and unearthed six Spanish coins bearing the dates 1782 and 1792. In October 1904 John Koonce of Dover, North Carolina, found a Spanish silver coin in very good condition dated 1708 at Fort Barnwell, Craven County.

Rum Story

In 1835 a story was told about a man in Orange County who came home one day with a keg of rum. He was immediately summoned to attend court as a juror and was greatly distressed what to do with his rum. It seems his wife was an intemperate woman and would surely find it even if he hid it. In haste he lashed a strap around the keg and suspended it from a beam in the house above the good wife's reach. The wife, who was lame and infirm, was supposed unable to get at the rum. After he was gone, she placed a large washtub underneath the keg and took a gun, held it underneath and pulled the trigger. The bullet pierced the keg, sending the liquor into the waiting basin.

The Great Honey Depression

In the 1930s, revenuers in western North Carolina not only fought to bring illegal alcohol production to a stop, but they also unknowingly helped save the lives of millions of honeybees. It seems that the sugar used in creating moonshine is of no use after a "run" so it is thrown out. The sweet crystal's aroma would bring the bees from all over the area. Unfortunately for the bees, it was like the "sirens calling to sailors at sea" to come and ultimately meet their death. It was not understood at the time whether the bees met their fate from alcohol poisoning or simply starved to death after leaving the heavenly heap and buzzing around in a daze, forgetting to eat again. At that time in the 1930s, it was estimated that at least three million bees had died because of the mash piles. A beekeeper from Black Mountain believed he had lost fifty thousand bees in the previous year and another from Chandler stated that he lost twenty colonies of bees estimated to number some thirty thousand honey makers. During World War II, sugar was hard to come by and moonshiners in eastern North Carolina used molasses and honey to sweeten their mash. Revenuers found it interesting that when they destroyed distilleries they discovered that the moonshiners would take a jar of molasses or honey, crack it like an egg and throw the honey, glass and all, into the fermenting barrels.

Plowed up Riches

In December 1884 a Mr. Jones in Buncombe County was plowing and pulled up an old oven containing $750 in gold and $250 in silver and some jewelry. In June 1915 B.B. Melton was plowing in Mooresville when his plow upturned a penny. He stooped down to pick it up and found others. This led to closer scrutiny of the soil and he found great clusters of pennies over a wide area. With the help of small boys, eighteen hundred to two thousand pennies were found. It was believed that the pennies were hidden from a post office robbery ten years previous.

Body Servant of Robert E. Lee

In 1914, there was a white-haired and polite black preacher named William McBee living in Gates County. At the age of twenty-eight, he was the former body servant of Robert E. Lee, carrying dispatches at the battle of the Wilderness and other engagements. McBee was educated for the ministry by means of $400 willed to him by Lee after the Civil War. By 1914, McBee had been a preacher for forty-eight years and had raised money to build his church by speaking of his interesting life in churches in eastern North Carolina.

Bear Hunter

In October 1889 peg-legged Bob Graham of Mecklenburg County, who had a reputation as a bear hunter, reported an unusual run-in with a bruin. It seems he was hunting in Yancey County and shot at a large black bear. He only wounded the animal and it charged at him. Bob stood his ground and extended his wooden leg out at the bear. It seized it greedily, and while he was chewing away on the wood, Bob reloaded his rifle and dispatched the beast.

Indian Cave

In February 1911 J.B. Blackwell and A.M. West of Alexander County were out exploring and discovered an unusual cave. It was located in Buncombe County, about five miles from Alexander County. The cave was situated among some steep cliffs and a rope was needed to get up to the entrance. It consisted of three rooms and looked as if it had not been occupied for a hundred years. The front room looked as if it were used as a kitchen, being strewn with grindstones and rocks hewn out like bowls. Connecting this room was a large room with walls darkened with soot, smoke and grime. The floor of the room was scattered about with arrowheads, axes and other Indian artifacts. A long narrow hallway connected this room with another one that was deposited with many skulls, bones and "skeletons packed away in place." The cave became a local destination for the curious.

Phenomenon in the Sky

In March of 1890 the skies over Watauga County left many with unanswered questions and fear. A remarkable circle manifested in the morning sky with what appeared to be four suns of equal distance and size inside. The phenomenon looked something like the planet Saturn because of the ring. The circle extended into the sun, then circled out north, south and west. The circle was composed of misty clouds and was well defined to the eye. The four suns in the ring seemed to be a massive ball of clouds and shone bright like a rainbow. The sky went unchanged until the early afternoon.

Goliath Rockfish

In the spring of 1813 near Bertie County, an unbelievable fish was caught at Mr. Underhill's fishery. It was a rockfish, or striper as some call them, which weighed upward of fifteen hundred pounds.

Two Fat Rattlesnakes

In early September 1873 near the township of Masonboro, J.G. Wagner, Esquire, and a boy were out hunting when they happened across a couple of large rattlesnakes. The boy saw them first and fired. The blast from the shotgun cut one of the snakes into pieces. Shortly after, seven smaller snakes about twenty-two inches in length slithered from the body of the dead snake. Mr. Wagner quickly dispatched the smaller snakes and then killed the other large snake nearby. The snakes were tied to a wooden cart and dragged to Mr. Wagner's house. Once home, he cut open the other snake only to see five more snakes crawl from the belly of the larger snake. The snakes appeared to be ready for battle, but again Mr. Wagner dispatched them like the others. The two large snakes were measured and found to be twelve and a half inches in diameter and each had eleven rattles and one button. About a week after the incident, a portion of the huge snakes was put on display at the Carolina House on Front Street in Masonboro.

Indian Relic

In February 1921 it was reported that G.W. Summerlin had unearthed an Indian idol or totem pole in a swamp near Dunn. The curiosity was found several feet under the ground and was made of a hard wood resembling resin-saturated pine. Believed to have been made by the local Chicora tribe, the idol had one eye, part of a nose and brow in perfect state of preservation.

A Few Mountain Superstitions

The lines that follow list some superstitions that folks in western North Carolina had in the late nineteenth century. One such superstition was that burning sassafras wood, looking at the moon over the left shoulder or through the limbs of trees was bad luck and an omen to the beholder. Another superstition said that in order to stop a wound from bleeding one must read a certain chapter in the Bible while walking around in a circle. One superstition about having a successful crop of potatoes, cucumbers and other vegetables was that you must plant them during a particular cycle of the moon. Another belief about food was that if you did your own butchering, you had to do it when the "sign" was right or your meat would turn to grease. And lastly, if it rains on the twenty-fourth of June, then there would be no mast (nuts on trees).

Revolutionary Fort

In 1890 an article appeared in a western North Carolina paper about an old log cabin still standing and apparently in good shape that was constructed around the time of the American Revolution. What made it so unusual at the time of the report was that it had several portholes around the entire cabin about midway between the ground and the roof of the structure. From the outside of the cabin all that could be seen were small holes just large enough for a gun stock to fit through, but the inside walls had large holes that gave the walls a funnel appearance. Apparently the large holes on the inside would allow a person to move in all directions from the inside in order to get a shot in any direction. The small opening also made it difficult for a bullet to find its way inside the cabin. The house was located about three miles from Salisbury on the Lexington Road and it faced the road to the Yadkin River, which Cornwallis marched over when pursuing General Nathanael Greene.

Alternative Use for Cottonseeds

In 1824 Professor Olmsted of the University of North Carolina discovered another use for cottonseeds after they had been extracted from their fluffy environment. He found that the seed could produce a gas that, when burned, gave off a brilliant illumination. The light was more brilliant than any source in use for lighting at that time. He reported that the amount of gas produced from a bushel of seeds was more than double that of the same quantity of New Castle coal. At that time, the new product brought excitement to those associated with it, because with cotton as a major crop in the South it would automatically provide an inexhaustible supply of seeds. It was believed that the seeds could produce enough gas to light every city in the United States as well as becoming a valuable export to other countries.

First State to Produce Gold

In 1799, gold was discovered in North Carolina in Cabarrus County. A gold nugget weighing seventeen pounds was found by a man named Conrad Reed. Years later, in the mid-1820s in the same area, a young slave boy found a nugget that weighed twenty-eight pounds. Most of the gold to be found in North Carolina was small, ranging from the size of a pinhead to a grain of rice, though larger specimens have been found. In 1824 at the Parker Gold Mine in Montgomery County, a nugget weighing four pounds eleven ounces was discovered by a small boy about ten feet underground. There is debate between North Carolina and Georgia on which state had the first gold rush. Both states however, were producing enough gold to warrant the government to open mints to produce gold coins beginning in 1838 and ending in 1861 with the start of the Civil War.

Smart Dogs

In 1874 near Wilmington, a young man headed for the woods to gather fuel. After filling his wagon he made his way home when one of the wheels on the wagon hit a stump. The wagon overturned, trapping the gentleman underneath. Unable to free himself, he called for help. No one came to his rescue except his dog. Thinking quickly, the young man took a handkerchief from his pocket and tied it around the dog's neck. He motioned the dog to go home and away he went. When the dog reached the house, a younger brother of the trap man spotted him. He knew there must be trouble once he saw the handkerchief and ran for the woods to help his brother. Fortunately, some foxhunters had come along to find the trapped brother and saved him from the predicament. The fellow suffered a broken leg, but he must have been mighty proud of the dog that brought help in case no one else came by. Another story of a brave a caring canine was reported in 1887 in Greensboro. The dog belonged to the Lou Reed family. Their house caught fire one cold winter night and would have probably taken the lives of the entire family had it not been for the heroics of the family dog staying outside. The pooch apparently sensed danger as the fire engulfed the house. It ran and jumped through a window to alert the family of the tragedy at hand. It was able to get their attention in time and avert a terrible death. The Reed family made it out alive because of the love of their dog.

No Place Like Home

In the fall of 1849 Blake Thompson left that part of Nash County that is now in Wilson County, and moved to Mississippi to live, taking with him his favorite dog. The following spring the dog made his appearance at his old home in Nash County. Mr. Thompson's father wrote him that the dog had returned on a certain day and it was afterward ascertained that the dog made the trip back from Mississippi in six weeks.

Old Gentleman

In the spring of 1877 a man named J.H. Lester living in Henry County, Georgia, was reported to be over 117 years of age. He was born in Nassau, North Carolina, in 1760. He was said to have fought in the War of 1812 and also fought for General Floyd in the wars between the Creeks and the Seminoles. He had three sons who fought in the Civil War.

No Free Ride

On a southbound freight train in the winter of 1888, Mr. Donavan Russell from the Lehigh Valley coal region paid an embarrassing fare to ride. Apparently Mr. Russell decided to catch a free ride on the freight train north of Charlotte. He made the trip in one piece, but just barely. After the train came to a stop in Charlotte, he crawled out from under one of the cars and proceeded to plead his case for a new pair of pants to the trainmen. He was wearing a hat, a coat and shoes, but was missing his pants. After being laughed at by the crewmen, he proceeded to tell his story. "I got on ther blooming trucks of that ther train something like forty mile above here to get a lift to Charlotte. I was sittin' on the brake beam, and what with swingin' on and holdin' up my legs to keep my feet from bein' clipped off by the cross-ties, I had about all I could 'tend to. Jest as I was doin' my level best to keep my grip on the beam, the train shot around a curve and I lost my balance. Then my blasted breeches got caught on the axle under me, and swip! zip!" The tramp snapped his fingers, threw his head to one side, kicked out his right foot, all with one movement and then continued: "The next minute my breeches was revolving around me at the rate of a million revolutions per hour. They were jerked off'n me quicker than a flash of lightning. The first stop that was made I tried to unwind them, but they come off in strings and wern't fit for anything but packing a hot box." After a good laugh the crew looked underneath the car to find his story was real. Out of pity for the fellow, they found him a pair of pants and took up a small collection for Mr. Russell so he could get a hot meal.

Three-year-old Pianist

In 1887 there was a remarkable story out of Reidsville about a blind three-year-old pianist. The child prodigy, named Henry Graves Early, was the only child of his parents, both natives of Rockingham County. He was exhibited in several towns in his area and had won local fame. Stories were told of him being wheeled in a baby carriage from house to house, and every piano in town was at his service. He could also play a tune on the German accordion if someone else worked the bellows. One day while visiting with his parents at the local sheriff's house, the sheriff's daughter played a popular tune on the piano. The infant, held at the time in his mother's lap, bent his head and with one hand to his ear listened intently. Then he sprang to the floor, and with outstretched hands toddled to the piano, exclaiming, "Et me play! Et me play!" They placed him at the piano and he played the same tune in perfect imitation of the young woman. It was said that that an offer had been received from Washington, D.C., to take the child and give him a musical education.

The Night the Devil Got Hezekiah Jones

This story, told in the 1950s by one of the witnesses, goes back to the early 1900s on Queens Creek, Onslow County. There was once a man named Hezekiah Jones who was a Confederate veteran. He was married several times and was very cruel to his last wife. She went blind and Hezekiah would torment her by tripping her and sticking her hand in boiling water. After his last wife died, Hezekiah was left to fend for himself since his relatives had little sympathy for him. But as time went on he became bedridden and his mind became deranged. People would come to care for him only to be startled when he would raise himself on his bed and scream bloody terror that the devil was coming for him. Finally he was believed to be on his deathbed and two of his young nieces came to his house to sit with him. The night the girls sat with him he remained motionless in his bed for hours and they knew it was going to be a long night. The girls then decided that since it would be a long night they would go out to the detached kitchen and make coffee. They made the coffee and returned to the one-room cabin. They had barely closed the door when Hezekiah again rose up on his bed and began screaming in torment, begging them to protect him since the devil was coming. Startled, they dropped the coffeepot and in their fright heard a strange noise outside. Hezekiah's screams and the strange noise outside made them cling to each other and crouch in terror in a corner of the room. The noise came up on the porch and sounded like hooves and dragging chains. They could not bear to look when suddenly the door exploded inward. They heard the hooves and chains come in the room amidst the horrendous screams of Hezekiah Jones. Just as suddenly as all this happened it got deathly quiet. The young girls shook in horror, waiting for what may come next. They heard the hooves and chains turn and go out on the porch and disappear into the night. They eventually heard the crickets and got enough courage to turn to look at what had happened. There on the bed Hezekiah Jones was sprawled out dead with a horrific look on his face. This was the night the devil came and got Hezekiah Jones.